THE
STORMS

Dedicated to Matilda,
Genevieve and Romilly,
and the memory of dear Louis.

THE STORMS

MIKE TRUEMAN

**bâton
wicks**

THE STORMS
Mike Trueman

First published in 2015 by Bâton Wicks.

BÂTON WICKS
Crescent House, 228 Psalter Lane, Sheffield, S11 8UT.
www.v-publishing.co.uk/batonwicks

This book is a work of non-fiction based on the life of Mike Trueman.
The author has stated to the publishers that, except in such minor respects not
affecting the substantial accuracy of the work, the contents of the book are true.

A CIP catalogue record for this book is available from the British Library.

ISBN: 978-1-898573-94-4 (Paperback)
ISBN: 978-1-898573-95-1 (Ebook)

Design and production by Jane Beagley.
Vertebrate Graphics Ltd.
www.v-graphics.co.uk

Bâton Wicks is committed to printing on paper from sustainable sources.

Printed and bound in the UK by T.J. International Ltd, Padstow, Cornwall.

CONTENTS

PROLOGUE

STORM AT SEA

Days when the shit hits the fan, more often than not,
start like any other day.

We set sail from Dale, on the south-west coast of Wales. The day was unremarkable; I vaguely remember some dampness in the air and the sun had yet to make itself known.

The water was calm as we moved gently out into the open sea. Astern, Milford Haven and its giant oil refinery, an incongruous sight on the otherwise naturally beautiful Pembrokeshire coast, slid slowly from sight. We would be fortunate to see land again.

I never sleep well on boats and in my half-awake melancholy, aided by the murky uninspiring scene around me, I was reminded that my previous knowledge of the area was through a story my father told about being refused permission to land the bodies of fellow seamen at Milford Haven, when he served in the Royal Navy during the Second World War. Death at sea, like in the mountains, is a very raw experience.

All around, the view was one of differing shades of grey. Even the land, before the sun illuminated its true colours, appeared in various dark hues and, ahead, softer shades of grey gradually blurred the sky with the sea, with no clear sign of the horizon. For the last two days a depression had been forming out over the Atlantic, but we felt we were well beyond its reach and, as we glided out to sea, we had little to worry us.

The yacht was a ten-metre Macwester Wight, a seaworthy craft with a centre cockpit. We were a crew of two. The skipper and owner, Dave, was my flying instructor on the army helicopter pilot's course, and he had asked me to help him move the yacht from Northern Ireland to my home town of Gosport, on the Solent. It was August 1979 and we were on our summer flying course break. I wasn't sure how much I could commit to the voyage because my wife was due to give birth in early August, but my son Tom arrived on time and, although I had missed the sail from Northern Ireland to Wales, I joined Dave on 11 August in the ferry port of Fishguard.

On 12 August we sailed down the coast to Dale, a small village with some 200 inhabitants and a very hospitable yacht club. Henry Tudor landed here in 1485 before the Battle of Bosworth, after which he became Henry VII of England. From Dale we planned to head out into the southern part of the Irish Sea, heading to Penzance on the south-west tip of Cornwall.

I was twenty-seven years old and had been in the army for eleven years. I wanted to follow in the footsteps of my father in the Royal Navy, but when his objections to that way of life became clear, I joined the army instead. Even so, I guess I still inherited his wanderlust and perhaps a career in the navy may have kept me out of trouble a little better than the army did.

There was not much work to be done on board. The weather conditions were favourable, the sails had been trimmed and we continued on a relatively straight course, away from the coast, out into the Irish Sea. I suffer from mild seasickness and prefer to remain above decks, particularly when the sea starts to roughen, and to make sure I can do this while being gainfully employed, I am happy to spend extended periods on the helm. Dave on the other hand was content to attend to the sails, cook the food and to navigate. We soon settled into a small, content team.

By mid-morning we were still surrounded by shades of grey murkiness and it did not look as if the sun was going to appear. If anything, the grey hue had become gradually darker as the morning wore on. We decided to have an early lunch and, as we sat there drinking our soup, we watched, almost with detached interest, as the sky changed from a dark shade of grey to inky blue. We were not unduly alarmed – this was, after all, the British Isles where the weather conditions frequently change and we were still optimistic that the changing sky was indicating nothing more sinister than a shower or two. There was certainly no thought about changing our plan to reach Penzance in one go and we happily sailed onwards, out into the Irish Sea, ever further from land and the safety of a harbour.

During the next hour, however, our pleasant day of sailing rapidly changed as the weather worsened at a pace that caused some significant concern. The sky continued to darken, menacingly, as if the sun had suddenly been eclipsed, and the previously placid sea started to simmer. It was not just the onset of bad weather that was giving us concern, it was also the speed with which we had to adjust to the worsening conditions. Within an hour we had gone from being on a relaxed cruise to having to cope with extremely heavy weather and it was getting worse by the minute. We put on foul weather gear and harnesses and shortened sail.

Dave was the skipper and the far more experienced sailor and I fully accepted any decisions he made. The yacht was without a radio (quite common at the time) and, therefore, without an up-to-date weather report, but with several hours of daylight left, we delayed any decisions about changing course until we were certain that what we were facing was more than passing heavy weather. The need for a quick decision, however, was forced upon us as the sky changed to a frightening, dirty black colour, and the sea changed from simmering bubbles to a churning mess in what seemed the same time it takes for placid water in a kettle to become a bubbling threat.

There was only one option – to be fair, given the direction of the storm, there had only ever been one option, even if we had taken the decision earlier. This was to run before the storm, from our position, which was by now well out into the Irish Sea, north-eastwards to reach shelter. Dave decided that Tenby on the south coast of Pembrokeshire, tucked in behind a small headland, would offer a safe haven.

An hour earlier I had been a participant in a pleasant sail, but now I was becoming concerned, although not yet frightened – that would come later. We were now at the mercy of the sea and enormous waves carried us forward until their acceleration overtook us and we fell down into a trough to await the pity of the next wave.

Nature is a powerful force. We surged forward, then seemed to hover before falling off the top of the wave into the trough, where we would stall as successive waves took their turns in taking a grip of the yacht before driving us forward. Each time we thought conditions could not get any worse we were proved wrong. We could only hang on and do everything we could to keep the yacht from turning sideways and broaching, which in such an almighty sea, could well have seen the end of us.

We neared the coast, some ten miles or so to the west of Tenby, but instead of giving us comfort, the visual reference of landmarks hurtling past made us appreciate just how fast we were moving in such a monstrous sea.

At this stage our feeling of concern changed gradually to one of fear. How were we going to stop? We were totally at the mercy of the sea and in such weather conditions there was no hope of gliding safely into Tenby's small harbour with its protective sea wall and tidal basin. We could only hope that somehow we could pick up an offshore mooring and ride out this huge monster of a storm.

Our opportunity to pick up a mooring off Tenby, in the lee of the headland, would need to come soon. The boat raced forward as we repeated over and over again a series of reactions that kept it pointing forward as each successive wave threatened to capsize us. We couldn't endure this much longer and we couldn't afford to miss the mooring. Unbeknown to us, out in the Atlantic off the coast of south-west Ireland, boats were going over, crew and lives were being lost.

Suddenly, we were sweeping past what we thought was a small headland, but which was actually Caldey Island, just before the small headland that sheltered Tenby. Ahead, after what was some five hours of hard sailing, but seemed far longer, we spotted the series of mooring buoys which lay several hundred metres out to sea from the small protected harbour at Tenby.

We were right – there was no chance that we would be able to get into the small, protected harbour, which was clearly being battered by the giant storm. Our only option was to pick up a mooring and ride out the storm – but this was easier said than done. Even with the headland providing shelter, the mooring buoys were being lifted through at least six metres as successive waves swept in.

David had long before taken over the helm and the plan was for me to hang over the bow, which was also swinging upwards and downwards through the same arc as the buoys, and to grab a mooring which I would then secure to the yacht. The only place I could successfully do this was at the bottom of the wave in the trough, where there would be slack in the chain holding the buoy to the seabed. The problem with all of this was that Dave had to make sure that my arms hanging over the bow reached the buoy at the moment when the bow and the buoy were both at the bottom of the trough. To do this, and to stall the boat long enough, Dave would have to turn into the wind at just the right moment.

The first attempt was a complete disaster as I tried to grab the buoy, only to find that we were suddenly surging upwards, which nearly pulled my arms out of their sockets and I started to think that picking up a mooring in such conditions would be impossible. Miraculously, however, we managed to pick up a buoy at the second try, but this was followed by a fearfully violent manoeuvre which threatened to capsize us as we and the buoy were lifted by the following wave and swung around into the full anger of the storm.

We had said little in the last few hours as the storm took hold. There was only one option open to us and, after we discussed what we were going to do, it only then required us to follow a simple plan, run before the storm and pick up a mooring. We hadn't planned beyond that, but we both knew by this stage that this was no ordinary storm and we were still a long way from feeling completely safe. All we could do was batten down the hatches and hope that we would survive the night ahead.

Sustained fear is like a long-term pain – you can learn to put up with it but you are desperate for it to go away. The intensity of the storm did not diminish. We were continually lifted, dropped and buffeted. I lost count of the number of bruises I received as I fell uncontrollably around the cabin. Sleep was not an option, but neither was tiredness – the fear was too intense to allow any retreat from full, alert awakeness.

At some stage a change of light indicated that day had broken and although the storm seemed to have abated slightly, on the grand scale of storms, ours was still a monster. We had, however, worked out that we had a limited window of opportunity when the tide would work in our favour to help us to escape this mayhem, by allowing us to enter the protective custody of Tenby harbour.

The plan to release ourselves from the mooring was similar to the one for picking it up, but this time, given that we were already attached, we mistakenly thought the process would be relatively easy. The bow continued to rise with the waves and then crash into the following troughs, and with David back at the helm and the engine running, my job was to reach down from the bow and release the line which attached us to the buoy. The yacht continued to rise and fall through an arc from the top of a wave to the bottom of the trough. At the lower end of the drop of the bow the pressure would allow me to release the line while David used the engine to keep us pointed into the weather to prevent us turning sideways and risking capsize in such a violent sea. This had to be co-ordinated and done in a matter of seconds before the next wave lifted us, and the buoy, and the chains lying on the seabed.

It was always going to be a lucky shot. There was not enough time for anything other than a perfect release from the buoy and as I started to cast off, and as David increased the forward thrust of the engines, we were lifted violently upwards towards the crest of a wave. The boat was now attached via my arms, which were the weakest link, to the seabed chain, and I was simply unable to keep us in contact with the buoy despite a scream from David telling me that I could not let go. Within a split second I dropped the buoy and, as the boat was thrust forward as the engine power was increased, the line which I had used to secure us to the buoy wrapped around the propeller. The engine stalled and without any propulsion we were now at the complete mercy of the monstrous sea.

David instantly reached for an emergency flare which he released skywards. There was no other option; we needed help. We were mentally exhausted and time seemed to stand still as we hung on and prayed as the merciless sea churned around us. It seemed an age but it was only a matter of minutes before our prayers were answered, as out of the storm a lifeboat emerged. The crew must have been waiting to be called as the giant storm battered the area.

My most vivid memory of the moment the lifeboat arrived was when a member of their crew armed with a pair of giant bolt croppers leapt onto our foredeck and immediately started cutting through anything which would prevent a towline being secured. I also recall thinking that he knew exactly what he was doing in order to sort out the situation. We had involuntarily experienced some of the worst conditions the sea could throw at us, but these brave volunteers who quickly took control of our predicament willingly put their lives at risk. Lines were cut and a tow secured and we soon found ourselves being pulled mercifully towards the inner sanctum of the harbour.

The storm continued to rage for much of that day outside the harbour walls, before it gradually faded. Over the next two days we repaired damage to the yacht and to ourselves before setting sail again.

In the same storm, the yachts competing in the Fastnet Race had been battered. Twenty-four yachts were abandoned, five sank and fifteen lives were lost. Of the 303 boats in the race, a quarter turned over and another third were knocked far enough over for their masts to touch the sea.

We had been very fortunate.

1

DESKBOUND:
MOURNING AND ANGRY

It is better to travel well than to arrive.

It was late May 1996, seventeen years after the Fastnet storm. I had returned from an expedition to Everest to my office in Hong Kong, where I was working as a corporate communications manager in the giant container terminal, a job which allowed me to take part in at least one major expedition each year. Waiting for me was that all too full in-tray and its pile of unopened mail.

I felt very odd. Just over two weeks earlier I had been involved in the co-ordination of a rescue on Everest after a storm had hit the mountain. Eight climbers had died. The events of that day were still making worldwide headlines and many of us who had been there were coping with daily requests from the press to give our personal views about what had happened. I had already given television, newspaper and magazine interviews and I was totally fed up with explaining to people, who had absolutely no understanding of mountaineering, what it was like to cope with events on the mountain during such an extreme storm.

I tried very hard to concentrate. It seemed so unreal, sitting there in my sterile office, clean-shaven, wearing a shirt and tie, and reading correspondence which ranged from complicated and urgent issues to junk mail and trivia. I couldn't help thinking about the families of those who had died on Everest, who would still be coming to terms with the deaths of their loved ones. To me they had been friends and climbing companions, but to others they were much closer: nappy changers, children, lovers, and breadwinners, not dead frozen tissue which would in some cases act as route markers for future generations of climbers challenging themselves on Everest.

Someone had sent me a postcard, which was a welcome change from both the serious and the routine mail.

I glanced at the picture on the front and, without fully comprehending which mountain it showed, I idly flipped it over. Was this some joke? There was Rob Hall's signature, staring back at me, but Rob was dead, and his body was lying somewhere near the summit of Everest. Three members of his team had also died on our side of Everest, along with another expedition leader, Scott Fischer.

The message was brief. It stated, actually boasted, that Rob Hall's commercial climbing company, Adventure Consultants, had been successful yet again in guiding clients to the top of the world. It went on to encourage the reader of the postcard to join Adventure Consultants if they too wanted to achieve success on future expeditions.

It was obviously not a joke and my emotions simmered, then boiled, into anger. How could anyone be so crass? People die climbing Everest, but here was a company so confident that they would achieve success that they had pre-written postcards to advertise the feat to encourage others to join them on future expeditions. I was particularly incensed that the postcards had been sent in the brief time between Rob getting to the top and him becoming trapped with his client, Doug Hansen, not far below the summit. Was it so necessary and vital to get such news out so quickly, considering the time it would take the world's postal systems to deliver the cards?

This was the second postcard I had received from a climber who had died by the time the postcard arrived. My friend Peter Boardman had written to me shortly before his death in 1982, when he disappeared with Joe Tasker on the north side of Everest. But that had been different: Pete was alive when he wrote the card, still confident about the future, using the card to arrange to have a drink when he passed back through Hong Kong.

Had climbing now become a competitive business to such an extent that expedition organisers had started adopting aggressive marketing techniques?

For the first time since arriving back in the office, I turned on my computer, and pulled up my news service programme. I entered 'Rob Hall' and 'Everest' and double clicked the search button. Up came a report which I had not previously read, written by the doyenne of mountain journalism in Nepal, Elizabeth Hawley. The report mentioned Rob Hall's team's 'success' and the achievement of Taiwanese climber Makalu Gau. But there was no mention of the climbers in Scott Fischer's team and there were more of Scott's team than there were of Rob's on the summit that day. Was this simply an overconfident, pre-organised marketing ploy which had been assisted by the respected Hawley, whose report had been circulated before the facts were confirmed?

Hawley's report stated that two New Zealanders, two Nepalese, one Australian, one American and one Japanese had reached the top. Actually, two Americans, from Rob's team, had reached the summit on the afternoon of 10 May. More noticeable was the complete lack of any mention of any of the members of Scott Fischer's team, most of whom had reached the summit before the majority of Rob's team got there.

Elizabeth Hawley is a legend amongst high altitude climbing circles for her recording of Nepal mountaineering expeditions. Although she has never climbed a big mountain, her knowledge of the mountains of Nepal is second to none. If you are named as the leader of a mountaineering expedition you can be assured that not long after your arrival in Kathmandu – or on your return at the end of an expedition – Liz Hawley will have left a message at your hotel to arrange a meeting. Some climbers see the Liz Hawley interview as being a rubber stamp which proves that what they are intending to do is a worthy mountaineering venture. But unless you are amongst the world's climbing elite, the purpose of the interview is simply to add you, your team and the expedition to Liz Hawley's database.

My first interview with Liz Hawley was when I was leading an expedition to Annapurna II and IV in 1992. The interview served no benefit as far as I could see other than adding information to the database, and I didn't even get a thank you for giving up my time, which would have been better spent on last-minute logistics before we left for the mountain. I have since met Elizabeth socially and she is a charming and intelligent lady, but on many occasions I have ignored her requests to meet, simply because expeditions in my view are about people and emotions and this is something that Liz isn't in the business of recording.

A second report by Hawley, filed on the same day, said the team members had reached the summit at 8.30 a.m. GMT. This was 1.15 p.m. local Nepal time, over two hours before the second American team member, Doug Hansen, reached the summit. So the information must have been transmitted to Kathmandu sometime between 2.15 p.m. and 3.45 p.m. Nepal time.

By Elizabeth Hawley

KATHMANDU May 10 Two foreign-led teams scaled Mount Everest on Friday, one day after a Taiwanese climber died following a fall, the Nepal Tourism Ministry said ...

Two New Zealanders, two Nepalis, one Australian, one American and one Japanese reached the top first. It was not the first time that two teams had reached the summit in one day ...

New Zealander, Rob Hall, 35, a mountain guide from Christchurch who has scaled four other 8,000-metre (26,250-foot) peaks, led the 11-member first team, ministry officials said.

It was his fifth successful ascent of Everest.

The others who reached the top were Andrew Harris, 31, a climbing and skiing guide from Queenstown, New Zealand; Michael Groom, 36, a climber and lecturer from Brisbane, Australia; Jon Krakauer [42, a journalist from the United States]; and Yasuko Namba, 47, a courier service employee from Tokyo.

The climb made Namba the second Japanese woman to reach Everest's summit. The first woman of any nationality was Junko Tabei of Japan, who gained the summit in May 1975.

Why was it so important to get out this news, without even waiting until all team members had reached the summit? And why wasn't the success of Scott Fischer's Sherpa guides reported, along with the one Russian, seven American and one Danish climbers? Would it have made any difference if the news had been more accurately reported the following day? Had Rob Hall made a deal with Hawley?

My mind was still in distant Nepal, rather than in the far-removed urban world of Hong Kong. I felt so many different emotions. What was happening to the sport of mountaineering which I loved? I had seen nothing wrong with commercialism in climbing, which gave those with the necessary experience the chance to climb big mountains which had previously been restricted to the elite of the sport. But in one bound, a leap had been taken into something crude, and unwelcome – it had become more like a horse race. The report should probably have said, 'seven climbers made the top of Everest today, there were five fallers'.

Reading the report from Hawley while flipping over Rob Hall's postcard in my hand was perhaps, for me, the moment that I realised that mountaineering was no longer a pastime, for many it was becoming a business.

2

BOY SOLDIER

I joined the British Army as a 'boy soldier' at the age of sixteen in 1968. Some thirty-nine years later I was head of a United Nations team tasked to remove 'soldiers' of a similar age from the ranks of the Maoist army at the end of the civil war in Nepal. While my friends at the grammar school I had just left were enjoying their final two years of education, I was part of a hard regime which was 'beasted' from before dawn until well after normal people would have gone to sleep.

Most of the instructors who guided us through those embryonic days of our military service were experienced soldiers, well-skilled in passing on their knowledge, but there were the exceptions. The last post-Second World War conscripts had left the British Army in 1963 and in 1968 the odd instructor still relied on harsh bullying from this era to guide their charges.

I have few fond memories of those exacting days, except for the times, every three months, when we were given the opportunity to take part in adventurous activities. I canoed, climbed and went on a parachute course, but it was my experience at the Army Outward Bound School that was to have the most long-term effect. In those days we were graded on the course and I was fortunate enough to be given a rarely awarded 'A' grade, which was to have an impact on my career. It certainly helped to counteract the report I received at the end of my time as a boy soldier, which to some extent reflected my response to an ogre of an instructor. At some stage during most weeks of my last term, I appeared for a disciplinary interview in front of my company commander, on a trumped-up charge made by a particular bully of an instructor.

I knew a lot about the weapons of the British Infantry when I became an 'adult' soldier in 1970, but I knew very little about life outside of the army. I was naïve and rightfully failed a selection process to become an army officer, and this led to disillusionment with my chosen career. It wasn't, however, a case of giving a month's notice. Having 'signed on' for a number of years, the only way to get out of the system – and even this took many months – was to purchase a discharge and the army made sure that this was a very expensive option.

I transferred to an air despatch unit at Thorney Island on the south coast of England. This was the start of four very happy years, during which I changed from a disillusioned teenager into an ambitious adult. The unit was tasked with delivering supplies and equipment by parachute to forces around the world, and also with providing support during civilian emergencies, such as the distribution of food during the famine which hit Nepal in 1973 – a task I sadly missed.

In the early 1970s Britain's army was focused on operations in Northern Ireland, a necessary security role, but somewhat separated from the type of soldiering I dreamed of being involved in when I joined the army. The enemy could have been anyone who you passed on the streets of Belfast, a city hardly different from any other part of the United Kingdom. The extreme verbal abuse – which would have offended a sailor in Nelson's navy – from the mouths of children not old enough to go to school, through to elderly people older than my grandparents, was a sad reflection of the depth of hatred which existed in post-war twentieth century Britain. It would be years before I would experience a similar level of hatred in the war in the former Yugoslavia.

One of the tasks of 55 Air Despatch Squadron was to support Britain's Special Forces, and in the early 1970s the opportunity to be attached to an SAS squadron during the war in Oman's southern province of Dhofar was as emotionally exciting at one end of the spectrum as soldiering in Northern Ireland was emotionally depressing at the other end. I first went to Dhofar in 1971 when our crew of four was attached to G Squadron of the SAS. Our arrival was delayed because the enemy was firing at the airfield at Salalah, but we got down eventually after the guns defending the airfield located and destroyed the enemy.

This was Britain's secret war, unpublicised by the government of the day, fought against the tribes of the Dhofar province who had been encouraged to rebel by a Maoist group, the Popular Front for the Liberation of the Occupied Arabian Gulf. It was so secret that when two SAS soldiers were shot and evacuated to Sharjah, where they died, we were tasked to load the coffins, 'camouflaged' by a surrounding crate, and fly with them to Bahrain, where I last saw them as they were trundled, like any other piece of cargo, on a forklift from the aircraft to the hangar.

I returned to Dhofar in 1973 attached to B Squadron 22 SAS. By this stage of the campaign the SAS, and the local forces they led, had established bases across the mountains bordering the coast of southern Oman. This part of the world suffers from the 'Khareef', a seasonal monsoon which starts in June and lasts for some weeks. This weather system causes the mountains to be covered in cloud down to ground level for much of the time, which prevents daily supply flights to the small bases in the mountains. For a large part of the time I was located at a base called White City, which was usually reached by an easy thirty-minute flight in normal weather. During the Khareef it took two long days to get there, first on a flight over the mountains into the desert, then in a convoy led by vehicles designed to detonate mines, and protected by guns and overflying jet aircraft and, lastly, as part of a heavily armed foot patrol through thick fog with the potential for ambush at any time.

Our position was commanded by Fred Marafono, one of several Fijians in the SAS, and a giant of a man in both body and personality. A year before, two of these Fijians, 'Laba' Labalaba and 'Tak' Takavesi had displayed great courage at the Battle of Mirbat when a large enemy force attacked the coastal town. Nine SAS soldiers were largely responsible for holding off an enemy force numbering hundreds until being reinforced by G Squadron who had just arrived in Oman to take over from B Squadron. At the height of the battle Laba had single-handedly loaded and fired a vintage World War Two artillery piece. After Laba was wounded Tak volunteered to move hundreds of metres to the gun to support his friend. Together they continued to fire the gun at point blank range, until Laba eventually received a fatal wound. Propped up against sandbags and having been shot through the shoulder and stomach, Tak continued to fire his rifle at the enemy. For his part in the action Tak was awarded the Distinguished Conduct Medal and Laba was mentioned in despatches – many of his comrades believe this should have been a very well-deserved Victoria Cross.

A year to the day after the battle I was based at Mirbat, where I was responsible for the airfield operations. Having been soundly defeated a year before, the enemy didn't reappear, but as the anniversary dawned I was struck by an emotionally charged visualisation of the great feat of arms which had taken place a year before on that July day in 1972.

I had decided to make the army my career, which was a significant change from my period of disillusionment some four years before, and I applied again to become an officer. While waiting to attend the Commissions Board I was posted as an instructor to the Joint Services Mountain Training Centre, which was based on the windswept west coast of Wales. It was partly a result of my performance at my Outward Bound course in 1969, and of my participation the year before in the annual joint British/Italian mountaineering exercise in the Italian Alps, that I was able to secure this job. Every year a group of British army climbers would spend two weeks in the mountains of Wales or Scotland undergoing a tough selection process to decide who would then go on to spend three weeks climbing in the Alps with the Italian Alpini (mountain regiment).

As a keen climber this was a fabulous opportunity to spend weeks at the army's expense doing what I did most weekends at my own expense – it was a no-brainer. I had previously taken part as a relative Alpine novice in 1972, but in 1974 I was back as a climbing group leader. The Alpini were superb instructors and we were given their best to work with. Two of our instructors, Virginio Epis and Claudio Benedetti, were particularly noteworthy having become, in 1973, the thirty-fourth and thirty-fifth climbers to reach the summit of Everest, and it was this experience to climb with such outstanding mountaineers that moved my interest in climbing up another gear. It was also my first experience of just how fragile life in the mountains could be. I had led a steep but straightforward ascent on hard snow when the second climber, who I was belaying from above, slipped just short of my stance. I watched with horror as he fell down the slope, very concerned that I wouldn't be able to stop him falling and even more concerned about what would then happen to me because I wasn't overly confident about my belay. I soon had my concerns answered as my belay gave way and I rocketed out into space and then tumbled downwards before coming to an abrupt stop some twenty-five metres down the slope, overlooking a series of deep crevasses. The number three on the rope, who had been belaying from below, was fortunately a very experienced Alpini climbing instructor, whose strength and skill certainly saved us from serious injury, or worse.

Interestingly, there was a link between the 1973 and 1996 Everest seasons. In 1973 the Italians had used a Hercules aircraft to fly a helicopter into Kathmandu which they subsequently used to supply their expedition up to Camp 2 in the Western Cwm. During a rescue mission on 17 April the helicopter crashed, fortunately without loss of life, and its remains stayed in the Western Cwm until it was recovered in 2009. The next time a helicopter landed in the Western Cwm was twenty-three years later, in 1996.

During my time as an air despatcher I had spent my free weekends climbing on the cliffs near Swanage in Dorset or on the crags of Snowdonia, and to now be able to do this full-time and get paid for it was more than I could have wished for. All instructors had to be at least sergeants in rank and in one of the strange ambiguities of the British forces, my records showed that at the age of twenty-one I was a substantive lance-corporal, acting paid corporal and a local acting sergeant all at the same time.

It wasn't all about canoeing, rock-climbing and hill-walking in the Welsh mountains. The centre still ran the occasional outward bound course for boy soldiers. These lasted three weeks and although it could be the middle of winter, on the first day of the course and on the last day of the course all of the instructors had to run the mile to the beach at dawn with their groups, where they all had to submerge themselves fully in the Irish Sea before running the mile back to camp before breakfast. The students had to do this every day and, besides the first and last day of the course, only the duty instructor had to accompany the students on the other days. Oh how I hated the experience – if only the students knew what was going on behind my cheerful expression when it was my turn to lead them to the beach. I rarely slept the night before each brutally cold plunge and I have had an aversion to cold water ever since.

It was during my time at the centre that I met and became a friend of Peter Boardman, one of the greatest mountaineers of his generation. I was planning to climb with another instructor in Alaska and sought advice from Peter, who at the time was the national officer at the British Mountaineering Council. In 1974 Peter and his climbing partner Roger O'Donovan had made the first ascent of the south face of Mount Dan Beard, which was also the second ascent of the mountain. Pete had a generous personality and was always unassuming – seemingly embarrassed by the fame caused by his brilliance on a mountain. In September 1975 at the age of twenty-four he became, after Doug Scott and Dougal Haston, the third British climber to reach the summit of Everest, when he climbed the south-west face of the mountain with Pertemba Sherpa, who was also to become a close friend of mine in future years. Mick Burke also reached the summit on that outstandingly technical expedition, but sadly died on the way down. Of the other four who made it to the top, two more died in mountain accidents during the next eight years. Dougal Haston was killed in an avalanche on 17 January 1977, while skiing close to Leysin in Switzerland, where he was director of the International

School of Mountaineering. My friend Pete Boardman took over as director of the school until he too died in the mountains on 17 May 1982, when he and his climbing partner Joe Tasker perished while attempting to climb the north-east ridge of Everest.

In April 1975 my plans to climb in Alaska were cancelled when I entered the Royal Military Academy at Sandhurst for the start of what was then a six-month course to become an officer. Sandhurst was as tough as it was fair. All the instructors were carefully chosen to play their part in turning raw material into what we euphemistically called a 'chappie'. We called the warrant officers and non-commissioned officers by their rank and they called us 'sir'. Given that warrant officers were also addressed as 'sir' it did lead to some strange conversations between themselves and the cadets, but, as the traditional explanation goes, the difference between the two was when a cadet called a warrant officer 'sir', he meant it.

There were generally two types of cadets on the Standard Military Course, those who had already been in the army for some time and those who were fresh from school. In the first few weeks the old military hands had a significant advantage as those new to the military learned to accept its discipline, to polish their boots to a high gloss and to press their trousers to achieve a razor-sharp crease. This advantage, however, was eroded as the two groups progressed to learning the skills needed to command groups of soldiers, which was readily picked up by the often more intelligent former schoolboys than by those with previous military experience, who had to change from their previous ways of soldiering.

Sandhurst accepted overseas cadets for training by charging 'fees' to their governments. Many came to be schooled for future royal duties as leaders of their nations rather than to be turned into soldiers. Had they been British, many would have been sacked from the course at a very early stage, but Britain's need to retain good working diplomatic ties with certain governments and the additional income meant that many completely incompetent overseas cadets finished the course. I recall one afternoon when we were due to take part in a particularly tough cross-country competition: an hour before the start a Rolls Royce turned up with embassy staff to snatch a 'prince' away for duties at the embassy, to save him losing face by failing to complete the competition course.

I was sponsored to go to Sandhurst by the Parachute Regiment, but during my time there I became impressed by the soldiering skills of the Gurkhas, who were used to demonstrate military tactics as well as play the part of the enemy in exercises. When it came to the part of the course where we applied to join regiments, the Gurkhas became my first choice.

For me there was a huge contrast between the thought applied to training boy soldiers, and the science applied to training officers at Sandhurst. The training of the former in the late 1960s was often unnecessarily brutish and lacked finesse, which ignited my rebellious side, while the latter built on lessons learned over 300 years of producing officers, and was an environment in which I thrived. Fortunately, or unfortunately, I was awarded the Sword of Honour at the end of my course, the first former boy soldier to gain this prize, but it was, and still is, a double-edged accolade. On arrival in your regiment you are more closely watched and more is expected of you, when all you want to do is get on with learning the trade of being an officer.

The first task on joining 2nd King Edward VII's Own Gurkha Rifles was to learn the language, without which it would be difficult to command Gurkhas in peacetime, and almost impossible in war, when the need to communicate clear understandable commands in the heat of battle would be essential. The second task was to transfer from my working class background to a way of life which had changed little since the days of the Raj in India. Many of my fellow officers had ancestors who had served in the regiment well back into the nineteenth century in battles which impacted on the growth of the British Empire, while mine were toiling in the rigging of Royal Navy ships or trying to crawl out from the slums of cities in the British midlands. Most of my new colleagues looked beyond family background; there were some who could not, but this didn't overly bother me. I was in the Gurkhas, in Hong Kong, and a new and exciting way of life lay ahead.

3

LEAVING THE NEST

I wasn't a good helicopter pilot. If you have ever piloted a helicopter you were probably much better at it than I was, and if you have never been a helicopter pilot you would in all likelihood have done a better job than I did.

After commanding the battalion's reconnaissance platoon, I was posted to Brunei to instruct at the Training Team Brunei, which was the army's jungle warfare school. Along with another captain who was in the Royal Marines, I was responsible for delivering the jungle warfare instructor's course and, additionally, I ran the long range reconnaissance patrol course, for small groups of soldiers who would have to learn to spend weeks in the jungle without the close support of other troops. Most of our non-commissioned officers had served in the SAS and the school had a particularly relaxed but professional operating ethos. It was a very happy time which also saw the birth of my first son, Daniel.

I thrived in my new role, but I was young and adventurous. The Gurkhas were going through an unusually quiet period in their history; for political reasons they were not allowed to serve in Northern Ireland, although British officers were allowed to serve there with other regiments, as I had done in Belfast with the Royal Welsh Fusiliers. I needed a new challenge and I decided to apply to become an army helicopter pilot.

The selection course for helicopter pilots was in three parts. Initially candidates attended the aircrew selection board, which in the late 1970s was at RAF Biggin Hill, the famous Battle of Britain airfield just to the south of London, where the prospective pilot was subjected to tests which would be more familiar to modern day computer game players. There was also a very strict medical to go through. Then, for those who had passed the initial phase of selection, it was off to the Army Aviation Centre at Middle Wallop where the focus was on interviewing the candidate to decide if he was suitable – this was decades before female pilots were rightfully recruited. Most who got to this stage were found to be suitable and then it was off to the joint services psychiatric unit, which was the last remaining section of the large Netley military hospital near Southampton. This was not, as some suggest, to test whether or not you were mad enough to fly army helicopters, but simply to see whether or not you suffered from epilepsy. A few years before there had been a fatal accident when a helicopter coming into land with its headlight on had possibly caused a helicopter which was taking off from the same site to crash. One theory was that the light shining through the blades of the helicopter which was taking off had caused a stroboscopic effect which had caused the pilot to have an epileptic fit. As a result all applicants were tested by having electrodes connected to their skulls, then being made to lie on a bed formed by a rubber latticework while having a series of lights flashed into their face over a prolonged period to see if this would induce an epileptic fit. It rarely did and virtually everyone passed, but there was an apocryphal tale that one candidate was found to be so prone to having a fit that the staff took his car keys away and refused to allow him to drive away from the hospital.

The initial part of the flying course was fifty hours on fixed-wing aircraft and on our course this was the De Havilland Chipmunk which had gone out of production over twenty years before, but was still an ideal aircraft for fledgling pilots. The theory was that you could train virtually anyone to fly an aircraft, but the army did this within a strict timetable, and any students who didn't reach the required standard at each point in the course were immediately sent back to their unit.

We started with sixteen students, but by the time we finished the fixed-wing phase we were down to thirteen. We then moved to the rotary phase of our training and I very clearly remember the initial words of our ground school instructor who said that although he was going to explain how helicopters flew, this was contrary to his personal belief that such flight should be impossible.

Our first sixty hours were spent on the Bell 47, the aircraft featured in *MASH*, which was first produced in 1946 and was still going strong some thirty years later. In most respects it was a very easy and forgiving helicopter to fly, but it had one difficulty which had to be mastered before students went solo. Unlike later generations of helicopters which had automatic throttles that applied additional power when the collective lever was raised when lift was needed, the Bell had a manual throttle which had to be turned at the same time as the collective lever was raised or lowered. This was a very pleasurable phase of learning to fly because we were simply required to pilot the machine. Even so, we lost another two members of our course before this phase ended.

We now moved on to advanced rotary and the Gazelle helicopter for the final phase before becoming qualified pilots. This was a beautiful aircraft to fly, much easier than the Bell 47, and it is still in service over forty years later. There is a theory which applies to most learning processes, but is particularly applicable to the army pilots' course, that says you start with a certain capacity that you use up as the course progresses. When all of the spare capacity is used up, the student pilot simply is unable to take in more information at the pace required by the course. We now had to learn not just to fly a new type of helicopter in the tactical way required by the army, but also to monitor several radios at the same time, to control artillery fire, to direct jet aircraft, to reconnoitre enemy positions and map-read while flying a few feet above the ground at 120 knots. The pressures were too much for another three course members and by the time we received our pilot's wings we were down to eight from the original sixteen.

I loved flying the Gazelle and I assumed I would be posted to Germany. However, events earlier that year were to have an impact on my future. In February 1979, China went to war against Vietnam in response to the latter occupying Cambodia during the previous year. A significant number of the troops China sent into action were stationed to the north of the Hong Kong border, and into the vacuum caused by their absence flooded hundreds of refugees intent on getting to Hong Kong to seek a new life.

For much of the year Hong Kong was hot and humid, and often buffeted by strong winds which made flying through its mountainous terrain demanding, particularly for recently qualified pilots. I was the only Gurkha pilot in the Army Air Corps and it was felt that my ability to speak to the soldiers on the Hong Kong border, the vast majority of whom were Gurkhas, would be useful.

This meant I had to learn to fly the Westland Scout, an aircraft that had come into service nineteen years previously, with avionics many years behind the sophistication of the Gazelle which I had come to enjoy flying so much.

I now had my wings and, with the birth of my second son, Tom, I felt settled into my new flying career. However, my spare capacity, which was enough to carry me through the initial pilots' course, had been significantly depleted during the conversion to flying Scouts and I found this helicopter far more challenging to pilot than my passengers and I would have liked.

I arrived at 660 Squadron in Hong Kong at the end of 1979 when the operations to stop refugees streaming into Hong Kong were well underway. My first few flights were designed to acquaint me with the geography of the territory from the air and to familiarise me with some of the tasks I would be required to undertake. One of my very first flights nearly ended in disaster when I was tasked, by the officer responsible for my familiarisation, with picking up a trailer using the hook underneath the helicopter. Unbeknown to me, the fellow officer had chosen a very overweight container to test my skills. As we moved away from the pick-up site with the trailer slung underneath, it started to swing violently under the helicopter. Within a short time it was swinging up to level with the cabin on one side of the aircraft and then swinging back under and up to the level of the cabin on the other side, and at the extent of the swing it was putting significant strain on the engine and rotors. In the back of my helicopter the aircrewman was yelling for me to sort it out (in those days we only flew with one pilot in the front and an aircrewman in the back of the aircraft). It was fortunate that I had just come from the flying school, because I suspect that in a few years' time I would have forgotten how to respond to what was happening. I gradually put the aircraft into a tight turn and used the centrifugal force to stop the trailer from swinging, after which I gradually came out of the turn with the trailer staying in place. It worked and the aircrewman stopped yelling.

The next three years were spent primarily supporting the operations against illegal immigrants. We worked in shifts and patrolled the Hong Kong border at first light and before last light. The first few patrols were harrowing, as we hovered over the bodies of those who had drowned trying to reach a better life, using the down wash from our rotor blades to shoo away the dogs who were trying to feed on the bodies. Most days we found several bodies, but after the initial shock of seeing groups of bodies lying together where they had floated ashore, one became relatively desensitised to this grim sight. The only exception, which always tugged at our emotions, was seeing dead children lying next to adults in what we assumed to be a family group.

On one occasion I was tasked with going to a sector of the border which was manned by British troops to pick up a body. After an overflight of the area I failed to locate the body and I landed on the sea wall next to the British base to grab a quick breakfast. As I walked along the sea wall I passed a group of soldiers sitting with their feet hanging over the edge of the wall having their photograph taken with a Chinese man. I stopped and turned round to look again at what they were doing, to discover that the Chinese man in their midst was the dead body I was looking for, and the soldiers had propped the body up to take their group photographs.

I was just about to say something when their sergeant major rushed past me to lay into the soldiers for being so despicable, in a way that only a raging sergeant major knows how to do.

Illegals were often brought into Hong Kong by speedboat during the night and only the raiding craft used by the Royal Marines were fast enough to catch them. The marines, however, had the disadvantage that although they were faster than the Chinese boats, they would often lose them in the darkness. The response from our headquarters was to tell us to use our 'night sun', a powerful searchlight controlled by an aircrewman in the back of the helicopter, to follow and illuminate the Chinese boats, while the marines captured them. Although it was to become standard practice in later years, we unusually flew these operations with dual controls and two pilots in the front of the helicopter, one focusing on the flying and the other commanding the aircraft and operating the radios.

We waited on the arm of the jetty of the headquarters building close to the Star Ferry on Hong Kong Island, waiting to be called by the marines. When the call came we were told that a Chinese speedboat was heading for Aberdeen on the south side of the island, whose harbour was narrow with high ground and high buildings on either side, and with large electrical cables hanging across from one side of the harbour to the other. This was not an environment a helicopter pilot would readily go into at night-time. Our instrumentation was antique by modern standards and the only instrument which set us apart from the planes at the end of World War One was a radar altimeter, which told us how far the ground was beneath us, which our barometric altimeter also did. However, what it didn't do, which would have been far more useful in Hong Kong's mountains, was tell us how far in front of us was the rock face we were heading for in the dark.

We actually found the Chinese boat fairly quickly, but almost immediately after finding the boat, we entered low cloud, which is the last thing you want to do at low altitude in an unsophisticated aircraft in hilly terrain. We immediately climbed, praying that there were no hillsides or buildings in the way. If anything, the cloud got thicker as we climbed and we popped out in moonlight at 2,000 metres. All we could see was a wide unbroken expanse of cloud. We called up the control tower at Kai Tak, which was the old airport in Hong Kong, and asked them to find us on their radar, in the hope that they would be able to guide us down. Despite trying for several minutes they failed to locate us. By this stage we were starting to get a bit desperate. We had no idea where we were, or what lay under us, and we were starting to get low on fuel. We were very afraid, but the need to be so focused on trying to escape kept the fear under wraps; in such a situation all emotions, particularly fear, have to be blanked out, and the Scout needed all our efforts to keep it in the air. Time and again we circled over the sea of cloud, still begging the air traffic controllers to find us, trying not to watch the fuel gauge as it moved inexorably lower.

There may have been more holes dotted around us which we didn't find, but there was one special hole in the cloud that we did find that night. We didn't even need to discuss whether we were going to try and descend through it. The fuel was very low by this stage and we dived through the hole below us without any discussion. We arrived under the cloud above a small hill, fortunately well clear of buildings and wires, some fifteen kilometres north of where we had entered the cloud and only a short distance from our airfield. We landed and walked to the officers' mess, where I drank a glass of whisky (not my normal drink) in an effort to calm my very stretched nerves. I can't recall ever being so afraid, but I then travelled home to my family who remained blissfully unaware that I had thought I wasn't coming home that night.

During a Hong Kong search and rescue exercise I was tasked with locating dummies which were being used for the exercise to represent survivors and casualties, after which air traffic control, who were running the exercise, would send a larger helicopter to recover the dummies. Sweeping the area of sea I had been given to search, it didn't take me long to spot nine dummies around 300 metres from the shore. I radioed to Kai Tak, who were controlling the exercise, that I had found the nine 'bodies', only to be told to confirm the number of bodies. I repeated that I had found nine, to be then told that there were only three dummies being used for the exercise. What I had located was the drowned crew of a fishing boat who had by sheer coincidence floated into the exercise area.

One of the great things about a helicopter is autorotation, which means the rotor blades can be turned by the air travelling up through them when the helicopter is descending, if the engine stops. The pilot can still fly the helicopter in this state with the aim of finding a suitable piece of ground to land on. Although it is unable to ascend, the helicopter flies almost normally in this state, and during our flying course in the UK we would invariably end the flight by autorotating to the ground, in what was known as an engine off landing (EOL).

The Scout had short rotor blades and if, in a real emergency, the engine malfunctioned and stopped, the pilot only had some four seconds to put the aircraft into autorotation before the turning blades slowed down too much. After that, the wind travelling up through the blades as the aircraft descended would not be enough to make the helicopter controllable – in effect it would tumble out of the sky.

Landing safely after an engine failure first and foremost requires the pilot to realise that the engine has stopped – a problem for army pilots who wear large helmets to prevent, amongst other things, their hearing becoming damaged by engine noise. In the early years of the Scout there was a design fault which actually led to the accidental switching off of the aircraft engine, and as a result at least four aircraft crashed with the loss of life. Someone, in their wisdom, had designed a heating control lever which was identical to the lever which switched off the delivery of fuel to the engine, and to make it even more likely that this could cause an accident, the identical levers were placed next to each other in the same operating plane, offering the potential for the fuel supply to be switched off when the pilot was trying to change the cabin air temperature.

EOLs needed to be done into the wind, or at least very close to this direction. Unlike the huge field which was used during training in the UK, which allowed EOLs into whichever direction the wind was coming from, the single strip used in Hong Kong was twenty-five metres wide, which dictated that practice EOLs could only be done in two directions. Each squadron had a qualified handling instructor (QHI), and every month or so each pilot would fly with the instructor to practise how to handle the aircraft in an emergency. Our QHI was very experienced and had been a former display pilot and on one of my flights, on a particularly windy day, we took the Scout up high above the airfield to practise an EOL. There had been some doubts about whether or not the wind that day was within limits for EOLs but the Squadron QHI was always the captain of the aircraft when another pilot flew with him. The first 2,490 metres of the descent from 2,500 metres were straightforward: I simply glided the helicopter down and lined it up with the grass strip running along the side of the runway. All I had to do then was flare the aircraft by lifting the nose, which increased the rotor revolutions, then put the aircraft horizontal and pull the collective lever to apply some lift as we touched the ground to run along the grass to a stop. What actually happened was that, as a result of the wind blowing strongly from the side of the aircraft rather from the front where it should have been, my flare had little effect meaning we virtually fell through the last ten metres. At the same time the wind had lifted one side of the rotor disc which meant there was now a high point and a low point to the revolving blades and the low point corresponded to the position of the tail of the helicopter, which the blades duly sheared off. Bizarrely, because we were wearing the noise-protecting helmets, we heard very little of what must have been, from the outside, a very loud noise, and the QHI said over the aircraft intercom that we should flare a little later next time. Still not realising that anything was amiss, we started to wind up the throttle which did lead to some strange noises, while at the same time several people were running towards us waving their arms.

We got out of the helicopter to find the tail was hanging limply from the main part of the fuselage and was almost split in half, while the drive shaft which sat along the top of the tail had been flung some 200 metres from what was now a very sorry-looking helicopter. It cost £250,000 to repair the aircraft, which was a lot in those days, and EOLs were subsequently banned, much to the joy of my fellow pilots who bought me several drinks as a result.

I loved flying and felt that it was the best job in the army, but I didn't want to do it forever and I returned to the Gurkhas after four very enjoyable years spent as a helicopter pilot, mostly flying in Hong Kong during which time my third child Nicole entered the world.

I did manage to fit in some adventure during my time as a pilot before my return to the Gurkhas and I led an expedition into the jungle in Borneo to find the wreckage of a Belvedere helicopter which had crashed in the Fifth Division of Sarawak on 4 May 1963. The aircraft was carrying drums of a particularly volatile fuel and all the RAF crew and the passengers, which included three SAS officers and an SAS trooper and the MI6 head of station, were killed in the crash. The crash site was particularly difficult to reach after a long trek through the jungle. I, along with two Gurkhas and a local Murut guide, located the site and a memorial which had not been visited for almost twenty years.

Although Scouts were used in the Falklands campaign in 1982, the pilots were from UK-based squadrons, much to the disappointment of those of us who flew in Hong Kong at the time. Instead I found myself leading a group of Gurkhas and aircrew to climb in Japan, on an expedition which had been set up by Peter Boardman the previous year. While I was in Hong Kong, Peter occasionally passed through with mountaineering expeditions and we always met up for a drink. I also arranged on one occasion for a flight for Peter, Joe Tasker, Chris Bonington and Al Rouse to view the Hong Kong border with China.

Just before we left for Japan, Peter again passed through Hong Kong and I was invited to join him at a drinks party organised by Jardine Matheson, their Hong Kong sponsors. For some reason Peter and I decided to demolish a bottle of Drambuie as we sat in a corner catching up on life. Peter was going to attempt the unclimbed north-east ridge of Everest, together with Joe Tasker, Dick Renshaw and Chris Bonington, supported by Doctor Charles Clarke and my good friend Adrian Gordon, who was an ex-Gurkha officer.

Peter seemed his normal happy self and as always he gave a clear analysis of what lay ahead. He also talked about Hilary, who he had married two years before, and it was obvious that he had found the perfect partner who could also join him on his adventures around the world. It was, therefore, very strange for Peter to tell me that he thought he would die on the expedition. My emotions had been dulled by too much Drambuie and I mumbled some inappropriate response. Peter was thirty-one years old and was established as one of the great mountaineers of his generation, climbing routes that others could only dream of.

Pete and the team went to Everest and we went to Japan, where we immediately ran into problems. I had arranged the expedition months before and certainly well before General Galtieri invaded the Falklands, but the Japanese press quickly found out we had arrived. The next day the headlines read, 'Gurkhas use Japan to train for Falklands War', and this news featured prominently across the Japanese media. By this time we were en route to the mountains and when I got there I had a message to immediately phone the British ambassador in Tokyo. While I was talking to the ambassador, who fortunately had a very pragmatic approach to events and told me just to get on with the climbing we planned to do, helicopters were landing outside the mountain hut delivering members of the Japanese media. Unbeknown to me the Japanese sympathised with the Argentinians because the Soviet Union had annexed the Kuril Islands from Japan in the later stages of World War Two.

We did what the ambassador advised and got on with the expedition. I split the group into three smaller climbing parties and we rotated through a series of rock and snow routes. On the second day I led my group on a challenging snow climb which took most of the day and proved to be more difficult than I expected. The following day another of our climbing parties tackled the same route and in front of them were two Japanese climbers. Halfway through the climb one of the Japanese climbers fell, followed very shortly after by the second climber, who landed on his partner. Our group immediately climbed to their rescue and on arrival at the accident site they found the first climber to fall was already dead and the second climber was in a bad way. The team lowered the injured climber to a point where a helicopter could transfer him to hospital and also brought down the body of the dead climber. All this was witnessed by the congregation of Japanese media who had come to get a very different story. Of course, the Japanese knew we hadn't come to Japan to train for the Falklands and they were human enough to appreciate that a life had been saved and a body honoured. Our status changed from villains to welcome guests.

Most of the press flew back to Tokyo, but one enterprising television channel decided to recoup some of their expenditure by making a film about Gurkhas visiting Japan. I was asked by the film crew if the Gurkhas would dance for them, to which I replied that this could only be done if we had some alcohol to drink – the price of alcohol in a Japanese mountain hut would make a millionaire wince. But my ruse worked and enough alcohol was bought to create a very enjoyable party – and after a few drinks the Gurkhas wouldn't stop dancing.

In the days of the British Raj, Indian Army officers, including those who served with the Gurkhas, were sent home to Britain every few years for six months' leave; primarily to find a wife. This wonderful tradition still continued into the 1980s, whether an officer was married or not, and in 1982 I ended my time as an army pilot with a long period of leave back in England with my family.

4

EVEREST 1996

Because it's there.

Everest Base Camp, for those attempting the mountain from the Nepalese side, is located amidst a jumble of boulders on the side of a large glacier just after it flattens out at the foot of the Khumbu Icefall. The tents are pitched beyond the range of avalanches and rock fall, which regularly crash down from the neighbouring peaks.

Everest has been climbed in all of the seasons, but the easiest times to climb the mountain are during April and May, and during September and October, before and after the annual monsoon hits Nepal. During these periods Base Camp becomes a village with hundreds of inhabitants. The village is sausage-shaped, measuring about 800 metres from top to bottom and up to 200 metres at its widest point. Teams who arrive early tend to pitch their tents close to the bottom of the Icefall, while teams arriving late have to make camp at the lower end of Base Camp. It takes up to half an hour, before first light, for climbers to stumble their way through a maze of tents and guy ropes from the lower camps to the foot of the Icefall, where the climbing begins.

Situated at the lower end is the helicopter landing site. The strong down draught of the larger Russian-built helicopters, which sometimes come into Base Camp, would wreak havoc in a tented area, so the landing site is kept well away from the inhabited parts of the camp.

Base Camp is a mass of vivid colour. Most climbers have their own tents, where they make themselves as comfortable as possible while they are not on the mountain. These tents serve as a home from home, with photographs of loved ones, private libraries and boxes containing jealously guarded delicacies which are brought from home to be eaten in small amounts, to break up the daily diet of monotonous camp food.

There can be dozens of brightly coloured tents, festooned with thousands of prayer flags swaying in the wind, allowing the prayers which have been written on them to float up to the deities. Flags also hang from poles which point skywards from the numerous stone shrines forming the focal point of each team's area and where, at the start of the expeditions, a ceremony is held to seek spiritual blessings for the safety of the team members during their time on the mountain. For many this is the last opportunity to party before the serious business of climbing a mountain begins. The Sherpas serve up traditional brews with seemingly the sole intention of getting all members of the team very drunk. It is a fun-filled time, which can last several hours depending on one's resistance to alcohol poisoning.

The smaller sleeping tents are located close to larger dining and kitchen tents. The dining tents can be quite luxurious. In 1996, those teams with clients paying US$64,000 certainly lived well at Base Camp, where staff were permanently on hand to serve their clients with delicacies brought from up-market Western delicatessens. Some tents had heaters and most had electric lights with electricity supplied by portable generators. They also had communications tents where members of other expeditions were allowed to send messages to the outside world, but at a price. One expedition leader, Rob Hall, charged members of other expeditions $50 per minute to use his satellite phone.

Our dining tent was not quite up to the standard of the eating establishments in the expensive commercial expeditions. It was affectionately known as 'Ice Station Zebra'. We did, however, eat well, and I am not sure the extra luxuries enjoyed by other teams were worth their members paying an additional $40,000, which was the difference between what members of Rob Hall's and Scott Fischer's expeditions were paying and what each of our team members had to contribute to the cost of the expedition.

A long table, which seated up to twelve of us, ran down the centre of our dining tent. There were only rare occasions when all team members were in Base Camp at the same time and meals were seldom crowded occasions. At the far end there was a small radio cassette player which belched forth a complete cross section of music. Along one side we had the emergency first aid kit, the bookcase, and in the far corner the communications centre, which consisted of a laptop linked to the satellite phone. This was owned by the Danish members of our team and cost $10 per minute to use. Even this seemed expensive, but it compared favourably with the $50 per minute alternative.

Most climbers suffer from chest complaints on the mountain, and coughing up lumps of phlegm is a common occurrence. For decades, spitting has been banned in many countries around the world, because of the potential for spreading disease. Most climbers appropriately deposit their phlegm off to the side of the track. Despite having a doctor in our team advising against it, it became common practice for members of our 1996 team to spit on to the floor of our tent. This was probably another difference between teams paying $64,000 and our expedition. We did, however, have a solar panel charging system located outside our tent, whose thirst for sunlight was easily quenched by the intense solar rays found at high altitude.

Toilets are generally stone-built structures, about two metres in height, with a base of about one metre square. Four large flat stones form the rim of a hole into which a barrel is placed. The barrel is removed by a Sherpa who arrives from the lower valleys once a week to perform the task. Unfortunately it is difficult to calculate the exact need for this facility, and often the barrel has long been overflowing by the time the 'shit-Sherpa', as he is affectionately called, arrives to replace the barrel. It is common practice to shake hands when meeting Sherpas, but in the case of the shit-Sherpa, a simple 'namaste' and a wave sufficed.

It does require a delicate balancing act and a careful aim to use the barrel effectively – more than one climber has lost their balance and ended up with one foot in the barrel. Climbers who miss and hit the surrounding stones are hunted down and harangued by their fellow team members, until the offender agrees to return to the toilet with soap and a scrubbing brush.

Daily life in Base Camp starts well before sunrise, with the departure of climbers and Sherpa guides up the mountain. It is worth pitching tents away from the many paths, which wind their way through the camp, just to avoid the early morning noise of the departing climbers. Or more importantly as a precaution against them tripping over a guy rope and collapsing your tent.

For those who are remaining in camp, one of the cook boys brings tea round to the tents shortly after dawn, which is a pleasant way to start the day. Most members doze in their sleeping bags until the sun hits their tents, raising the temperature to an acceptable human level.

A gong (normally a metal plate struck by a ladle) announces breakfast. Most meals are Western in nature and Scottish porridge is a regular feature of breakfast. Other meals feature chipped potatoes, which are readily available in the Khumbu region. Climbers tend to lose their appetites at altitude and it is difficult to replace the additional calories that are lost during the climb, with most climbers typically losing about twelve kilograms during the expedition.

During the morning climbers visit other teams, wash clothes or themselves, or just laze around. Occasionally forays are made out on to the glacier. During one of these trips on to the glacier, I found the remains of a climber from some past expedition. Some bones remained, including the backbone, from which tattered material of his climbing clothes was still evident. The remnants of a leather boot lying close by suggested that the climber came from a 1950s or 1960s expedition, when traditional leather boots were still worn. For the remains to travel this far down the glacier must have taken at least twenty years. After lunch climbers usually seek the warmth of their sleeping bags as the afternoon gets cooler, and then sleep, read, or catch up with diaries.

The evening meal is generally eaten with climbers wearing duvet jackets and woollen headwear – at least it was in our dining tent which didn't have any heating. With the temperature well on the minus side of the thermo-meter, this almost al fresco experience – the tent making little difference to the temperature – is not the most comfortable way of eating a meal. This is followed by the hardier team members sometimes playing cards late into the night, while the more timorous of us seek the warmth of our sleeping bags as soon as the meal finishes. Some read by candles, others prefer to use their head-torches. There is plenty of time to sleep on exped-ition, and the lack of exhaustion at bedtime can mean long restless nights.

Life in camp is a mixture for some of rest and socialising. Most climbers give up drink during their time on the mountain, but this is not always the case, and sometimes impromptu parties last well in to the night. Sexual liaisons are not unusual. Perhaps it is the closeness of death and danger which encourages some to form relationships in a relatively short time in such a cold barren place. Marriages break up, long and short term relation-ships form – just like life in other villages throughout the world but conden-sed into a short period of time. But within Everest Base Camp it is difficult to meet secretly, and hurried meetings in tents soon become topics of gossip.

Our camp in 1996 was located in the middle of Base Camp, beside the main path leading to the Icefall and next to Rob Hall's team. Maybe Rob advised his team members against visiting other teams. Certainly in the six weeks or so on the mountain in 1996, I cannot recall many visits by our neighbours – if they visited at all. Rob did pass by, but seldom stayed for long, presumably preferring the comfort of his own camp to our compara-tively barren offering.

Our team title in 1996 was The International Everest Expedition, and we were climbing the Polish South Pillar route. This route shares the normal South Col route as far as the bottom of the Lhotse Face, where it splits and takes a direct line left up to the south-east ridge. The original South Pillar route took a harder and more direct line to the summit, but it has become more usual for teams attempting this route to join the south-east ridge closer to the South Col, where they follow the normal route to the summit.

In 1996 it cost $70,000 for a permit to attempt the normal route, but only $50,000 to climb any other route, including the Polish South Pillar.

Our team leader was the veteran Scottish climber, Mal Duff. Intelligent and tough, with a great sense of humour, Mal was a first-class leader and the ideal climbing companion. The majority of the expedition's members were experienced climbers, who paid Mal to organise the expedition.

Our team was made up of two Finns, four Danes and four British climbers. One climber had already left the mountain by the time I arrived at Base Camp having been 'scared off' by the hazards in the Icefall.

The Finnish climbers included Veikka Gustafsson, who had previously climbed Everest and K2. Veikka was an extremely fit professional climber, who was aiming to climb Everest without oxygen. The second Finn was Jaakko Kurvinen, a most likeable and capable climber with whom I would team up with later in the expedition. The Danes were really a sub-team in their own right and were all experienced climbers who had previously climbed together on several occasions around the world.

The other British climbers, alongside Mal and me, were Ginge Fullen, a professional diver in the Royal Navy, and Euan Duncan, an officer in the Royal Air Force with relatively little expedition experience. The British Army had climbed Everest in 1976 but there was still a desire in the other two armed services to achieve this feat. Ginge had paid for himself to come to Everest and his motivation and desire to get to the top was admirable, whereas Euan had been funded largely through support from the RAF.

I had great confidence in the ability of the Finns, Danes and Ginge Fullen, and under Mal's leadership I felt we had a realistic chance of success.

Our support team was led by our Scottish Base Camp manager, Mick Burns. Well-travelled and full of wicked mischievous humour, Mick was a great companion at Base Camp. Not all teams have a Base Camp manager, and those that don't leave the organisation of their support team to their Nepalese sirdars (the head Sherpa). The Base Camp managers have their costs covered, but are usually unpaid. Staying at Base Camp, for up to eight weeks, can be extremely stressful, particularly when team members are injured or killed on the mountain. Certainly, as far as our team was concerned, having Mick Burns to look after matters at Base Camp while we were on the mountain was a bonus.

Mick worked closely with our climbing sirdar, Kipa Sherpa, allowing the latter to focus on requirements on the hill. Like most sirdars, Kipa was a multiple Everest summiteer and one of the very few Sherpa guides who had climbed the technical south-west face of Everest. He was a burly, tough Sherpa with a sharp sense of humour who was well respected by all of the team members.

Kipa was supported by a team of ten Sherpas, including the two who were dedicated to maintaining the route through the Icefall. There is very little physical difference between the Sherpas who work for the teams on the mountain. They are generally all extremely strong and fit, with natural wit and intelligence. Promotion within the Sherpa hierarchy generally goes to the more worldly-wise, outgoing Sherpas who demonstrate leadership.

The second most important Sherpa in a team is the cook. Most of the seasoned cooks on Everest are able to conjure up the most amazing dishes with very basic ingredients. Quite often these cooks demonstrate similar temperaments to those exhibited by head chefs in leading restaurants around the world.

The cook is supported by the cook boys, who are employed to do the daily unskilled tasks around Base Camp. In 1996 we had two cook boys who, like the cook, worked extremely hard throughout the expedition. They were up at 4 a.m. every morning to light the stoves and prepare the breakfasts for the team members who were moving up the mountain. Their next daily task was to deliver tea and coffee to the members who were, that day, resting in their tents. They did this whatever the weather – which could on occasions be extreme. They would then act as waiters during all meals, as well as being on hand to prepare the numerous drinks which members require during their time at Base. The most physically demanding task for the cook boys was collecting water from the glacier which had to be done several times a day.

One of the cook boys always wore yellow waterproofs, rather like those worn by firemen. Both he and his trousers seemed to get dirtier and dirtier throughout the expedition. He was nicknamed 'Baldrick', after the man-servant in *Blackadder* – a very apt title.

Base Camp in 1996 was a truly international arena. At the bottom of Base Camp were the South Africans and the Yugoslavs. I had spent eighteen months in war-torn Yugoslavia between 1992 and 1994. I had lived, during the war, in several parts of the former Yugoslavia, a complex, but beautiful and passionate land and I felt at home with both Croats and Serbs. The Yugoslav team was made up mostly of climbers from Monte-negro – an area of Yugoslavia of which I had become particularly fond. The team members were always hospitable and it was a pleasant excursion to walk down to their camp. They had brought with them a significant quantity of their national brew and it took a great deal of persuasion and diplomacy to leave their camp in the upright position.

Phuri, their sirdar, had been my cook on an expedition I had led to Anna-purna IV in 1992 and it was particularly pleasing to see that this immensely strong Sherpa had gained promotion during the intervening years.

The South Africans were equally hospitable – provided that their leader, a complex character called Ian Woodall, was absent during the visit. I first came across Woodall in the late 1980s when I was working at the British Ministry of Defence in London. Woodall was a Territorial Army lieutenant in the Royal Army Pay Corps (a position he held for three years before he resigned – although he was later to make some very bizarre claims about what he did during this period) and he had put forward a proposal to lead a team to climb Everest. I was asked by my senior officers in the Ministry to meet Woodall and to make an assessment of his suitability to lead an Everest team. Woodall had co-opted Mal Duff to be his civilian adviser and the three of us met in a bar in Chelsea in London to discuss the proposal.

I questioned Woodall about his climbing background and in my view he didn't have the necessary experience to either lead or take part in an Everest expedition. I then checked further with his Territorial Army superior, before making my report to the Ministry which concluded that Woodall shouldn't be allowed to take the proposal any further. An expedition by the Territorial Army to climb Everest in winter did take place in 1992, and included Mal Duff as a guide, but without Woodall.

I was very surprised when I found out some eight years later that a South African newspaper, the *Sunday Times*, had sponsored Woodall and that here he was in 1996 leading a high-profile attempt on the mountain, an expedition which had the support of Nelson Mandela. In order to get the sponsorship, Woodall had claimed to be an experienced mountaineer, as well as putting forward claims about service in the South African and British military, claims which I thought were inflated from the evidence of my previous meeting, although that had been some years earlier. Even though they were agreeing to sponsor the expedition at a cost of tens of thousands of US dollars, the senior staff at the *Sunday Times* did this without either verifying his claimed mountaineering experience, or his military service. This failure would later cause a PR disaster that would haunt the newspaper in the years ahead.

On arrival in Nepal, team leaders are required to meet with the mountaineering section of the Ministry of Tourism to finalise the paperwork and confirm payment of the peak fees before setting off for Everest. At the meeting the names of those who are on the permit, and thus allowed to climb above Base Camp, are also confirmed.

Woodall had selected strong South African rock-climbers to be part of the team, including Edmund February, who was credited with hundreds of new rock-climbing routes and had, a few years before, proved good enough to feature on the front cover of the respected climbing magazine *Mountain*. Also on the team were Andy de Klerk, another leading South African rock climber with a penchant for BASE jumping at the end of a climb, and the experienced alpinist Andy Hackland. He had also included the British scientist-turned-photographer, Bruce Herrod. With degrees from both Oxford and Cambridge, Bruce was a very intelligent individual who had previously worked with the British Antarctic Survey.

It was assumed that the others on the permit were to be Cathy O'Dowd and Deshun Deysel, both of whom had applied along with 200 other female South Africans to compete for two places on the expedition. The two of them were taken as part of a final group of six women to the mountains of Meru and Kilimanjaro in Tanzania for the final selection. It later transpired that not only had Deshun been left off the permit, but Ken Woodall, Ian Woodall's sixty-nine-year-old father, who was later to join the team at Base Camp, had been put on the permit.

By the time I got to Base Camp over half of Woodall's team had mutinied or deserted, claiming that Woodall was too authoritarian. These included the doctor, Charlotte Noble, who according to rumours around camp had been sacked by Woodall for giving medicine to sick locals, and the three experienced male South African climbers, Edmund February, Andy de Klerk and Andy Hackland, who had decided that they couldn't work with Woodall. This must have been a particularly hard decision for the three of them to make, given how much an opportunity to climb Everest must have meant to them, but it also reflected how far relationships in the team had broken down, at such a relatively early stage in the expedition.

I acknowledge that Everest is not a technical mountain, but it is enormous, and in my view requires experience gained over years to ensure that those who attempt it are able to look after themselves in extreme conditions. Cathy O'Dowd had limited mountaineering experience and had only applied to take part in the selection process four months before the departure of the team to Nepal. Deshun Deysel had also applied at the same time, without any previous mountaineering experience.

Deshun was a beautiful and intelligent black South African. She had been selected to go to Everest by entering the competition which Woodall had organised to select two female climbing members for the team. He had stated that only one of the two female team members would actually go above Base Camp and the final selection would be made when the team arrived at the foot of the mountain. Rather an odd and potentially dangerous selection given that Deshun had no snow and ice experience. It was also rubbish to claim to select climbers at Base Camp, because all climbers have to be on the permit to climb higher than Base Camp and this is finalised before teams leave Kathmandu.

The plot thickened when Woodall's father turned up at Base Camp and it became apparent that Deshun had never been on the permit. Woodall's father was a rather gruff man in his late sixties and he had great problems just making it to Base Camp – there was no way he was going to be able to go any higher. At $10,000 for an individual's share of the permit, this did seem to be an expensive waste of the funding provided by the *Sunday Times*, and at the expense of Deshun who had gone to the mountain believing that she would have the opportunity to fulfil her dreams.

The editor of the *Sunday Times*, Ken Owen, and his wife later trekked in to the mountain, but after an explosive meeting during which it was reported that Woodall threatened 'to bury' the Owens, the *Sunday Times* formally withdrew its sponsorship, arguably a bit late since most, if not all, of its money had already been spent.

There were two other odd teams at Base Camp – one from Norway and the other from Taiwan. The Norwegian team had one member, Petter Neby, who intended, together with his Sherpas, to climb the south-west face of Everest. This route is normally in condition in the post-monsoon season, when a covering of snow makes some sections easier to climb. In 1996 the route was well out of condition with constant stone-fall, making progress exceedingly difficult. It didn't take Neby long to appreciate the foolhardiness of his attempt, and after two or three weeks he abandoned Everest. This solo expedition was estimated to have cost well over $150,000.

The Taiwanese were an accident waiting to happen. They had started their project with a disastrous attempt on McKinley in 1995 by a team of seven climbers. During the attempt, one climber was killed and several others ended up with frostbite, which reduced their numbers to the two members who formed their Everest 1996 team. It became clear from the start that these two climbers lacked the necessary experience. This caused alarm amongst the other teams who understood that such a lack of experience would more than likely result in an accident, which the rest of us would be expected to respond to.

The cast were in place, but the drama was yet to unfold.

5

A DANGEROUS PLACE TO LINGER

Waking at 4.30 a.m. in a cold tent on a glacier at the foot of the world's highest mountain, with over a thousand metres of climbing ahead, can be miserable. The climb begins in the dark, in the clinging cold, followed by sweltering sweat-producing heat once the sun has hit the slopes. Lying there, slowly awakening, thinking about what lies ahead, can be daunting.

We use very warm sleeping bags on Everest and it takes an enormous effort to drag one's sleep-drugged body out of the comfortably warm cocoon to face extreme cold, exhaustion and some danger. I always prepare by sleeping in most of my climbing clothes. Personal morale is low enough before dawn in the cold damp darkness of the tent without having to struggle into layers of damp mountaineering gear.

Most of the final layers of clothing are put on in a half-asleep, zombie-like state, but boots and gaiters are always difficult to sort out. The fingers seem to lose their feeling whatever precautions are taken. The rucksack is also normally pre-packed and carefully checked the night before. It is particularly difficult to search for essentials in the brain dead period preceding dawn.

Exiting the tent is a further miserable experience. Breathing through-out the night produces vapour which freezes into a thin coating of ice on the inside of the tent. Opening the tent inevitably causes a sprinkling of ice, which always finds a naked patch of skin. This can be much worse if it has snowed during the night. The snow has an amazing ability to penetrate into remote parts of the body in the same way that sand does during a day at the beach. Exiting from the tent is followed by a stumble to the kitchen to get some welcome hot liquid into the system. The cook boy will have been up hours by this stage, and his cheery greeting is difficult to respond to.

Around the kitchen, Sherpas and climbers sit in the darkened, steam-filled gloom, bent over, with hot drinks firmly clasped in two hands in an effort to gain the benefit of whatever heat the drink is throwing out. No one seems to want to say much. None of these huddled figures looks like they will be physically capable, in a short time, of taking on the turns, twists and dangers of the Khumbu Icefall. The Icefall is so-called because, like a waterfall, the frozen ice flows out over the lip of the Western Cwm down to the valley below.

All too soon it is time to move on, to gain as much height as possible before the sun hits the slopes. Although the cold is extreme, it is easier to climb in such low temperatures, rather than the debilitating heat that can be generated once the rays of the sun strike the ice.

It can be a stumbling walk of over twenty minutes in the early morning blackness to reach the start of the Icefall, particularly for those teams whose camps lie at the bottom end of Base Camp. Some climbers use head-torches to guide their way through the maze of tents, others just stumble, head down, seemingly dependent on some invisible guidance system. Frequently, the early risers trip over tent-supporting guy ropes, much to the annoyance of the tent's occupants, who still have another two or three hours of rest before a cook boy brings early morning tea.

One irritating Sherpa in 1996 would chant Buddhist mantras whenever and wherever he went, including on his pre-dawn journey through the middle of our camp.

On leaving the tented area the route becomes confusing. It is only a short journey on the right path, but climbers frequently go astray, with further damage to their morale. It can be really annoying to become lost so close to camp. Small piles of rocks – cairns – mark the route, but these were placed in the bright light of day. Even during the day, finding the way through this short section of the route is very difficult, and finding the way in the dark is another matter entirely.

At the foot of the Icefall, a small crowd usually forms as climbers stop to put on their crampons and climbing harnesses. Some exchange greetings, but most go about their task in anonymous silence. It takes some time to complete the job of putting on the gear. Sleepy brains and cold fingers mean that simple tasks can, on occasions, become minor epics, as buckles and fasteners seem to refuse to do that for which they were designed. Then it is time to move unrelentingly upwards, through the mass of beckoning dangers.

The lower section is generally easy-angled and provides an opportunity for climbers to warm up and flex cold, cramped muscles. Some of the small cliffs and snow ramps in the lower section of the Icefall are fixed with rope. There are, however, few dangers in this area, and the benefits of these ropes are doubtful.

During that first hour or so the brain gradually clears, as much as it is able to in the oxygen-depleted atmosphere above 5,500 metres, particularly during the initial stage of an expedition when climbers are still trying to acclimatise. This early part of the upward journey becomes a trudge in a semi-conscious state. Almost in parallel with the increasing light of the day, the brain gradually awakens, and the climber becomes aware of and grows to appreciate the sheer magnificence of the Icefall and its surrounding features.

Some climbers prefer to travel on their own – I certainly do – whilst others seek the company of groups of various sizes. There are also the long lines of Sherpas, constantly moving supplies to the higher camps. There is not much opportunity for conversation as the climber moves progressively upwards, and daydreams of family, home and friends help to pass the time. There is plenty of time to think on a mountain.

The sprinters among the climbers are quickly well clear of the pack and forge ahead out of sight. Amongst the remainder there is little overtaking as the line of climbers starts to spread. Most climbers prefer a steady plod up the Icefall. There is little physical benefit to be gained by overtaxing the body.

All too soon it is time to cross the rickety aluminium ladders held together by blue polypropylene rope. Some are not too rickety, whilst others bend, sway and tilt at amazing angles. On either side of the ladders, other blue polypropylene support lines, attached to anchor points, attempt to keep the bridges firmly in place.

Below the ladders, enormous and seemingly bottomless crevasses split the lower section of the Icefall at the point where the ice starts to flatten out and turn left at right angles to join the Khumbu Glacier on its journey down the valley to become a river and reach the sea.

Each climber wears a sit harness, with two loops for the legs, attached to a belt around the waist. At the front of the belt there is normally a loop, through which is clipped a karabiner, to which two tape slings are attached. At the other end of each sling are two more karabiners.

On either side of the aluminium ladder bridges, there are two safety ropes into which the climber clips each karabiner, which are at the ends of his two tape slings. The safety ropes are attached to anchors on either side of the crevasse, and if the climber falls off the bridge he should be left hanging to the safety line. I don't know anyone who has completely fallen off a bridge, but I equally don't know anyone who wants to try it. The spikes of the crampons on the climber's boots usually fit neatly between the rungs of the ladder-bridge, and the snugness of the fit gives an added feeling of security.

Some climbers, when confronted for the first time with the bridges of the Khumbu Icefall, are unable to cross standing upright. Instead they bend over on all fours and adopt a strange crab-like posture. Others crawl across on all fours. Some climbers never get used to the bridges and always cross in this manner.

About eleven metres is regarded as the height where humans are subject to the optimum appreciation of vertigo. Below that height the effect of altitude diminishes and above it the level of fear is relatively constant, whatever height one looks down from. Most crevasses in the Icefall are far deeper than eleven metres and more often than not they appear bottomless. It can be unnerving to see Sherpas regularly crossing these bridges without clipping in, or, in some cases, without even holding on to the safety lines.

Sherpas are often seen in the Icefall without crampons and, in some cases, just wearing trekking boots. In 1996 I first met and spoke with Lopsang Jangbu Sherpa in the lower part of the Icefall. In my diary I noted 'one Sherpa, with a ponytail, wearing jeans and training shoes, told us he was returning from Camp 2. He was 23 years old and already climbed Everest three times without oxygen.' In six months this charismatic Sherpa would be dead, having been swept off the Lhotse Face by an avalanche.

The route through the Icefall is never boring and no two features are the same. Each major feature is given a name, for easy reference, so that climbers can give their positions by radio to their base camps, receding below them. In no time at all, Base Camp becomes an ant-like colony, far below.

In 1996 we had the 'popcorn', where boulders of ice rested on each other, like corn in a packet at the cinema. Then we had the 'football field', where, with a bit of imagination, the ice seemed flat and large enough to play football on. Then most alarmingly we had the 'mousetrap', where climbers had to move up left to right on a ramp, below an overhanging cliff which tilted each day further and further out from the vertical, making the ramp almost a tunnel by the end of the expedition.

If the climber needs to go to the toilet, it is just a matter for male and female alike to move off to the side of the track. There is no room for shyness between sexes on the mountain, and everyone quickly gets used to this uninhibited lifestyle during their time on expedition. Having a 'dump', as it becomes affectionately known, is a little more complicated, primarily due to the climbing harness and the layers of clothing which have to be removed in the process. It is also considered poor form to leave piles of crap lying close to the climbing line. Many of these actions and processes, which become habitual during the climb, have to be rapidly forgotten when climbers return to civilisation.

Most of the Icefall is fixed by rope, which is anchored at regular intervals. The anchors are formed by snow stakes – long aluminium pickets which are hammered into the ice, or by ice screws – short metal spikes which can be screwed (if they are ones with a screw-like thread running around the outside) or hammered into place. Climbers clip one of the karabiners from the slings attached to their harness into the rope and if they slip then they, in theory, will only fall as far as the next anchor point.

In 1996 it was Mal Duff, along with his team of Sherpas, who established and fixed the route through the Icefall. Mal's team had arrived in March, several weeks before the arrival of the expeditions, to complete this task.

Once the route is established, it is the job of two Icefall Sherpas, nick-named the 'Icefall Doctors', to carry out daily maintenance. Every day they travel up and down the Icefall, checking anchor points and securing bridges. Often, the collapse of an ice cliff or the opening of a new crevasse means that the route is completely changed. Rarely will climbers make the journey up through the Icefall more than five times in the course of an expedition. These two Sherpas, between March and the end of May, will complete the journey through the Icefall more than sixty times.

It takes about four hours to climb the Icefall in the early stage of the expedition. Later, when the body becomes more acclimatised, this journey can be done in three hours. The sun has reached most parts of the Icefall by 9 a.m., so unless the climber has started particularly early, all will feel the effects of intensifying heat at some stage during the climb. And it does get hot. From temperatures well below zero in the pre-dawn darkness, it can get up to around thirty degrees Celsius once the sun has moved overhead.

As the climbers move upwards they become aware that the landmarks seen in the distance from Base Camp are now much closer, clearer and larger than they appeared from far below. The climbers soon reach the level of the Nangpa La, the pass to the left of the Icefall which leads to the northern side of Everest and from where George Mallory looked into the Western Cwm of Everest in the early 1920s and gave the cwm its name. Nuptse to the right seems so close, and Pumori, behind, seems less gigantic.

Sometimes avalanches fall from the slopes of the west ridges of Everest, up to the left, but fortunately these avalanches fall well clear of the route, which has been specifically planned to bypass the danger zones. Sadly, this was destined not to be the case for all future expeditions.

Several ice cliffs have to be climbed during the journey to Camp 1. The less vertical are ascended by pulling up the rope with a jumar – a clamp attached to the end of one or both of the tape slings. It will move freely up the rope, but lock on to the rope if it is pulled backwards. If the climber falls, the jumar should lock and leave the climber dangling from the rope.

Traffic jams on the lower part of Everest are not common. It is normally quite easy for climbers who are descending to move past those who are on their way up, and on some cliffs there is an up rope for jumaring, and a down rope for abseiling.

The steeper cliffs can be difficult to ascend, particularly in the early part of the season, before the passage of many climbers leads to the formation of staircases of large footholds, and if you have a heavy pack it adds to the difficulty. Sometimes the ropes hang well free of the cliffs, making it necessary to use two jumars. This can be particularly exhausting near the top of the Icefall, just below Camp 1, where more often than not the sun's rays are hitting the slopes by the time climbers reach this point.

For the really high cliffs, the same kind of aluminium ladders which are used to form the crevasse bridges are lashed together and placed up against the ice. Some of these vertical ladder sections can be over eighteen metres, and several ladders lashed together do not make a rigid structure. There is an added fear factor as the cliff to which the ladders are attached gradually leans over from the vertical as the climbing season progresses.

The Icefall has a fearsome reputation, but fortunately careful route-fixing and management has reduced the number of accidents in this section, but would not, as we were to learn, prevent future catastrophes. There are times, however, when the climber considers what would happen if a crevasse should open and suck them in, or if a cliff collapses, dumping tons of hard ice on to them, crushing their bodies. In the mountains death is rarely instantaneous. Climbers can have their life grasped from them if they are hit by rockfall, in whatever fraction of a second it takes for the body to realise that it is dead, but more often than not death is a slow process – sometimes very slow. Death in an avalanche, in a fall from the side of the mountain, or death by cold and exposure, can all give a climber at least enough time to know what is happening before life is extinguished. More often than not the one line in a newspaper, reporting a climber's death, could be replaced in reality by a page of painful detail describing how it really happened.

Of all the sections on Everest, the Icefall does provide some technical challenge and I enjoy its variety. A number of climbers have been known to take one look at the Icefall and then leave for home. For those, however, who persevere, it can become an enjoyable climbing excursion, particularly once the body has acclimatised and the ice can be climbed with less and less physical effort.

The top of the Icefall is normally marked by a high cliff, because this is the point where the glacier flowing out of the Western Cwm starts its journey downwards – just like the lip of a waterfall. It is also a dangerous area; despite Camp 1 being a short distance away, there is no room for complacency. The movement of the ice over the lip can lead to the formation of hidden crevasses, waiting to suck in the unwary climber. The ice at this point can easily detach itself from the glacier it has been part of for hundreds of years – a further danger.

The change in scenery at the top of the Khumbu Icefall is quite distinct. One moment, climbers are hauling their way up a vertical cliff, the next moment they are standing on the edge of a mountain Shangri-La, the Western Cwm of Everest.

6

RESCUES IN THE ICEFALL

Days on Everest when people are injured or die start like any other day. Such news arrives at any time and it quickly circulates around Base Camp. It is discussed and forgotten. We all know the risks, and the grieving process is better left until the expedition is over.

On 20 April 1996 I awoke early at Camp 2. I had been suffering from an altitude-induced headache and I wanted to get back in order to recover in the thicker air at Base Camp.

I left camp at around 6 a.m. and for a short time I seemed to have the Western Cwm to myself. On my right side towered the south-west face of Everest and, on my left, looking equally large from my viewing angle, stood the north face of Nuptse. Small, early morning avalanches tumbled silently down their slopes, but how wonderful that power looked in such an otherwise tranquil setting.

The descent route took me first down a short gully, where I turned left at a junction marked by a dead body wrapped in a blue plastic cover. Who he or she was, or how he or she got there, no one knew. The person had become an anonymous climber, who had at one time arrived at Base Camp with the same desires and ambitions which I had when I arrived seven days before. It was also not clear why the body had been left at this point in the middle of the Western Cwm. Perhaps bad weather had hit whoever had been carrying the body downwards. Later that season the body was finally taken down.

There are many bodies on Everest. Some are hidden in unknown resting places, following falls, and others can be seen, but cannot be retrieved, while some are high, and to bring them down is unrealistic. But there are others which can be reached and brought down and gradually the mountain is being cleared of its grim relics.

From where this body was resting, the route swept out on to the gently descending floor of the Western Cwm. On the descent the bamboo marker wands which mark the route were passed far more quickly than they were during the crawling ascent twenty-fours hours earlier. At the top of each wand were red flags, which helped to indicate the route in poor visibility. On that day they hung limply in the windless morning air.

After 1,500 metres or so the route passed close to Nuptse before it meandered through the crevasses of the lower part of the Western Cwm. A few ladders acting as bridges had to be crossed between there and Camp 1. These too were included in the daily maintenance schedule of the Icefall Doctors, who had the day before turned up at Camp 2 for lunch, having begun their work from Base Camp well before first light.

From my view down to Camp 1, I could see climbers starting the short, but tiring, journey up to Camp 2. These climbers were the first I had seen that day. Their relative size in contrast to the surroundings demonstrated the vastness of the Cwm and the sheer size of the mountains on either side.

Camp 1 can be anywhere in the lower part of the Western Cwm. In 1996 we placed our camp very close to the top of the Icefall. This appeared sensible to me, because after the exhaustive climb up from Base Camp, it was only a short stumble to the tents to seek rest and recovery. Other teams chose to put their camps higher up in the Cwm, to shorten the walk to Camp 2. The highest camp in 1996 belonged to Scott Fischer's Mountain Madness team and, on reaching their site, it was still a kilometre or so down to the start of the Icefall.

Just before the lower camps, the route skirted under the slopes of the west ridge of Everest, before cutting back left at right angles across the top of the Icefall. Here there were some more precarious bridges. This section of the route changes more than other parts, as the ice speeds through a narrowing gap between Everest and Nuptse to plunge over the lip to the valley below.

Without stopping for rest that day I continued on downwards with an increasing feeling of well-being, as the thickening oxygen started to have an effect. Just below the top of the Icefall, I stopped to talk to Ginge Fullen who was making his way up to Camp 2. Ginge was a British Royal Navy diver who had been awarded the Queen's Gallantry Medal when he rescued lorry drivers from the car ferry, the *Herald of Free Enterprise,* when the ship capsized moments after leaving the Belgian port of Zeebrugge in 1987. He was a fairly quiet man, but I liked his obvious sincerity. I bade him bon voyage as I continued my downward journey.

The journey down from Camp 2 to Base Camp took three hours, and I arrived in time for breakfast with my fellow team members. Not long after my arrival, Mal received a radio call, and gave me the shocking news that Ginge Fullen had suffered a suspected heart attack near the top of the Icefall, presumably moments after I had passed him. Some Sherpas who were with him at the time were bringing him down and other climbers and Sherpas resting at Base Camp left to go and assist with the rescue. Given the circumstances, they took some oxygen cylinders with them.

Through binoculars we watched as the procession slowly moved back to Base. Fortunately, Ginge was able to walk for short distances, but it was clear from the number of rest stops that he was very weak. We could see two descending climbers who appeared to overtake the procession. This did seem strange, because in such a situation any help would be welcome, particularly if Ginge collapsed and had to be carried down.

It later transpired that one of the climbers was Charlotte Noble, formerly the doctor on the South African team. After being sacked by Ian Woodall during the walk-in, an event which led to the mutiny by most of the South African team members, Noble had continued up to Base Camp. To climb above Base Camp requires climbers to be on a recognised expedition permit, and if they are not on a permit the penalty is severe. Noble was not on a permit and rather than use her professional medical skills to assist in Ginge's rescue, she decided to pass by quickly, one assumes to minimise the risk of being caught illegally climbing in the Icefall. Noble was probably unaware that so many eyes were looking upwards and the jungle drums beating at Base Camp had already notified the Nepalese liaison officer that there was a problem. Climbers often turn a blind eye, but when a fellow climber in trouble is ignored, particularly by a doctor whose help would have been particularly appreciated, justice is quickly dealt out. When Noble arrived at Base Camp, she was met by the senior Nepalese liaison officer who gave her hours to vacate camp, failing which she would be fined $10,000, the cost of each climber's share of a permit to climb Everest.

Meanwhile, the party bringing Ginge down was making very slow progress. Crossing the bridges was causing significant delay, because Ginge had to rest each time to ensure that he had the strength to make the short crossing in safety.

Late in the afternoon the party arrived at camp and Ginge was placed in a tent where he was cared for by Caroline Mackenzie, the doctor with Rob Hall's team. There are normally several doctors dotted around teams on Everest. Some are specialists, and Ginge was lucky that Caroline was able to seek advice over the radio from heart specialist Stuart Hutchison, who was high on the mountain at the time.

The doctors were very concerned about Ginge's condition and an early evacuation by air was needed. I tried to reach Kathmandu using the large satellite phone in our dining tent. It was, however, Saturday in Kathmandu when most businesses are closed and, despite trying several numbers, I was unable to contact anyone.

I then decided to phone my wife, who was a doctor working with the Gurkhas in Hong Kong. I knew that she would have the number of the duty officer at the British Gurkha barracks in Kathmandu. Ginge was, in any case, a member of the British armed forces and such a request would receive priority assistance. She phoned me back some time later to tell me that she had spoken to an officer in Kathmandu and a helicopter would arrive at Base Camp first thing in the morning.

Ginge passed a difficult night and there was a growing concern for his condition. At first light he was carried down to the helicopter landing site. Seeing him lying there, wrapped in a sleeping bag and breathing oxygen through a mask, it was difficult to imagine that he was the same person, full of ambition, who I had met at the top of the Icefall only twenty-four hours earlier.

Ginge had to wait for almost three hours at the landing site, but just before 9 a.m. we heard the wasp-like drone of the approaching helicopter. Fortunately, Ginge recovered and was able to continue his venture to climb the highest mountain in every European and African country, a feat he accomplished in 2005.

The following week the British armed forces public relations team in Hong Kong decided that the story of this rescue may be of interest to a wider audience and they issued a press release to newspapers in the UK. It was, therefore, with a great deal of alarm that a week later my sons, Daniel and Thomas, and daughter Nicole saw an article in a newspaper with the headline 'British Climber Suffers Heart Attack on Everest', with a picture of me below it. Fortunately, it became apparent that my picture was there because of my telephone call to Hong Kong to arrange for the helicopter.

Bizarrely, the story achieved wide coverage within the British press, who were misleading readers by saying that I had made the phone call using a mobile phone and several of the articles were accompanied by pictures of well-known brands of mobile phones. Most headline writers seemed to see this as a heaven-sent opportunity to make full use of their headline writing skills. My favourites were: 'Off-peak Call Saves Climber', 'High Love, I Am Stuck Up Everest' and 'Summits Up' – the latter typical of the UK's *Sun* newspaper.

On 30 April I was at Base Camp having a rest when the news came through that one of the Danish members of our team, Kim Sejberg, had fallen in the Icefall. It was not exactly clear what had happened. He had been found lying in the snow by climbers from the IMAX team, who were a group of world famous climbers making a film of their ascent of Everest. Together with our Base Camp manager, Mick Burns, Finish climber, Jaakko Kurvinen, and some of our Sherpas, I climbed up to help Kim get back to Base Camp.

Trying to climb quickly through the Icefall to assist an injured climber is a particularly exhausting and painful experience. By the time we reached Kim we were all wrecked and it took a while for us to recover sufficiently to be of any use. Fortunately the Austrian climber, Robert Schauer, who was a member of the IMAX team, had stayed with Kim until we arrived to take over the evacuation.

Kim had suffered broken ribs, a badly damaged knee and cuts to his head. But most significant was the look on his face, which showed very clearly the extent of his devastation, having realised that his injuries were sufficiently bad for him to have to abandon his attempt to climb the mountain. Kim was in great pain and each step was its own nightmare journey. His accident had happened about 300 metres above Base Camp, right in the middle of the Icefall.

On the descent, we had to stop frequently. Kim was becoming more and more exhausted, and was clearly on the verge of collapse. Supporting him across the bridges was becoming a significant problem and I doubted that we could reach the bottom of the Icefall before nightfall.

Eventually we staggered into camp, and Kim at last received the much-needed medical attention. We had lost two team members in a fairly short time – both in relatively unusual circumstances and relatively low on the mountain in the Icefall.

7

PRELUDE TO TRAGEDY

Wednesday 1 May 1996 was my forty-fourth birthday, and Everest Base Camp is a memorable place to spend a birthday. My teammates had organised a party and it was a pleasure to relax and take my mind off the impending attempt to reach the summit.

Two days later, on 3 May, I left Base Camp at 5.30 a.m. to start the long flog up to Camp 2. I climbed with my partner, the Finn Jaakko Kurvinen. We had become fully acclimatised during the previous four weeks and this was my fourth trip up the Icefall. Each ladder and hazard were by then very familiar to me. In some ways it made the climb seem longer, because I knew what was waiting around the next corner, but we reached Camp 1 in three hours, which was ninety minutes faster than the first time I had climbed through the Icefall.

We managed to get to Camp 1 before the sun started to drench the Western Cwm with its hot, penetrating, strength-sapping rays. I was, however, suffering yet again with diarrhoea and I had to make a short stop at the camp.

It brought back unpleasant memories from three weeks before, when I was stuck on my own at Camp 1 while a storm struck the mountain. As I lay in my tent, praying that it would not be blown off the mountain with me inside it, I started to feel very sick. I crawled out of the tent into the raging blizzard. I wanted to vomit at one end, while at the other end extreme diarrhoea was having a very unpleasant effect. With my trousers around my knees, with brown liquid coming from one end and projectile vomiting spraying out on the wind-blown snow from the other, I felt that life was being a little unfair.

Three times I crawled out into the snow, but the weather was getting worse with 100-plus-kilometre-per-hour winds having some disturbing effects on my exposed parts each time I took my trousers down.

I could face it no more and I searched for the largest cooking pot in the tent to solve my sad predicament. I had never appreciated just how much crap the human body can hold, but, by early next morning, I had managed to fill the large cooking pot. The storm had gone and I knew that the first Sherpas would be arriving from Base Camp at about 7 a.m. At 6 a.m. I felt exhausted, but otherwise much better than I had done some hours before. I stuck the pot outside and in the intense cold of the early morning, the contents took only a few minutes to freeze solid. I leaned out and around the side of the tent and a simple tap on the bottom of the pot dislodged a deep, perfectly round, solid brown disc, which I quickly covered with the surrounding snow. I then filled the pot with compacted snow, which I intended to bring to the boil to clean out the pan. Just as it reached boiling point, the first Sherpas arrived, and there followed a quite difficult moment when I pretended that I didn't understand their request for boiling water to fill up their tea flasks. To bring an end to what was becoming an increasingly difficult conversation, I pretended to trip, and knocked over the pan of boiling water in the process.

Now, three weeks later, Jaakko and I felt very strong, despite my stomach problems, as we continued upwards. The Western Cwm opened ahead of us and, as I glanced up towards the summit, I kept daydreaming about reaching those lofty heights within the next few days.

The route from our Camp 1, at the top of the Icefall, ran initially for about 100 metres across the top of the cliff formed at the point where the ice of the glacier started its downward plunge. There were two bridges there to be negotiated. In this area the sudden change in the direction of the ice flowing out of the Western Cwm, and the resultant increase in speed of the flow, causes the glacier at this point to buckle, split and implode. Each time I went up there a new crevasse had appeared, or the existing holes in the ice had dramatically changed shape since my previous visit. It was essential to take great care when crossing the bridges in this area.

The route then swung diagonally right across the lower reaches of the Western Cwm, to reach a point under the face of Nuptse. This area was also heavily crevassed, but our path was well-established and the more dangerous points were marked by crossed bamboo poles, each with a red flag on top.

The sun had risen sufficiently for its heat to penetrate this high valley. The rays reflected and bounced around the steep-sided cwm, and our bodies started to warm up rapidly. We stopped to strip off our clothing at regular intervals. We also applied thick layers of sunscreen to fend off the effects of the sun's rays striking our naked skin.

I was wearing a white floppy hat, which I had bought when I was a spectator at a cricket tournament in Hong Kong. It was ideal protection against the sun, although I did look a bit odd – but then so did many others. The more experienced climbers had their own specially designed head-gear, which they wore for practical reasons, rather than to look good in expedition photographs. There were many who wore baseball caps, with handkerchiefs stitched to the back, making them look more like members of the French Foreign Legion than high-altitude climbers.

Some also had water bottles with long straws strapped to the shoulder straps of their rucksacks, which allowed them to drink on the move. The water, however, tended to freeze solid during the colder periods of the climb and to me the system had limited appeal. It is vital to maintain a healthy fluid intake in the hot, energy-sapping microclimate of the Western Cwm. I preferred to use vacuum flasks, even though they weigh more than the lighter plastic bottles – at least they guaranteed that the liquid contained therein would remain unfrozen.

From the foot of the Nuptse face the route ran diagonally to the left in the direction of Camp 2, which was at the base of the giant south-west face of Everest. This is the longest straight stretch on the mountain – the route runs endlessly ahead, like a long, thin Roman road. Every 200 metres there is a bamboo marker. With our heads down we tried to put our minds in neutral, placing one foot in front of the other to bring us closer to our destination. I would look ahead to the next bamboo marker and play a game with myself, trying to resist looking up until I reached the marker. I would then start the game over again. Such is the glamour of high-altitude climbing. It was very common to pass exhausted climbers lying in the snow. Even the fittest could suddenly wilt in the heat of the cwm.

Just before we reached the point where the body was lying to the side of the track, just below Camp 2, the diarrhoea struck again. While I sorted myself out, Jaakko moved ahead. The sun continued to make its presence felt and I suddenly felt very weary. Looking ahead I could see Jaakko, also tiring visibly.

From the body the route turned slightly right, to run parallel to the south-west face for 400 metres, up to Camp 2. I have always found this part of the climb completely exhausting. In those 400 metres that day, I stopped at least ten times. Each stop was a collapse in the snow, with my pack still on, until my mind and spirit were prepared to haul my body to the next point of submission.

We both crept into Camp 2 and collapsed in our tent. But this gave us no relief. The temperature that afternoon was thirty-five degrees Celsius and it was impossible to cool down, inside or outside our shelter. We stripped to our underpants and lay in our tent, which felt exactly like a sauna. Within two or three hours the temperature would be down to at least minus twenty degrees Celsius, perhaps even lower, a variation of more than fifty degrees Celsius in a matter of hours.

Lying there like fish out of water, we saw the two Spaniards returning from an unsuccessful summit attempt on the South Pillar route. They were a cheery pair and I was sorry that they had not been successful, but I couldn't help but harbour the thought that we could now be the first to succeed on the route that year.

Camp 2 on Everest becomes Advanced Base Camp for all the expeditions as their team members become more acclimatised, and it is almost an exact copy of Everest Base Camp. There are large dining and cook tents and the area is bedecked with prayer flags, all carried by the Sherpas. The only difference is that there are fewer smaller tents, as climbers are forced to share accommodation to ease the logistics. The tents are pitched on several levels and it can take up to fifteen minutes to stroll from one team's area to another.

It is at Camp 2 that some of the infamous rubbish that litters Mount Everest could be found. Unlike Camp 1, which has no annual fixed location, Camp 2 is always placed in the same area. Here and there, signs of previous expeditions from years gone by were readily visible. Old non-biodegradable trash was most evident, with the odd oxygen cylinder lying about. The Sherpas are now paid a bonus for bringing down the old cylinders, particularly from the South Col, where there had been, not long previously, hundreds to be found. Although there were still piles of rubbish dotted around, the situation was significantly better than it had been in the past, mainly due to legislation imposed by the Nepalese. A deposit now has to be paid by each expedition, which is returned when it is proved that the expedition has brought out from the mountain a pre-determined amount of rubbish.

Next day we sat and waited. The weather was clear, but above us there was a harsh grating noise as the jet stream continued to batter the mountain, as if someone was using a loud hairdryer. When the jet stream flows over the top of Everest, it is not safe to attempt to reach the top. Sooner or later the jet stream will move to the left or right of the summit, where it will continue to flow without any obstruction. This is the time when summit attempts can begin in earnest, before the track of the jet stream moves again, back over the top of the world's highest mountain.

On 4 May, two other members of our team, Veikka Gustafsson and Bo Belvedere Christensen, arrived at Camp 2. They planned to climb to the summit with Jaakko and me, but they were not intending to use supplementary oxygen.

The four of us lazed around in the afternoon heat, listening to the constant screaming noise of the jet stream buffeting the mountain above us. One of the games we played at Camp 2 that year to pass the time was to spot a geostationary satellite which could be seen with the naked eye when the sun reflected on its surface.

Critical to our plan was the setting up of Camp 4 on our route, but because of the continuing, unsuitable conditions, it had not yet been established. We discussed the various options open to us. It seemed to be sensible to delay for a couple of days, with the possibility of going to the summit at the same time as the IMAX team.

Sunday 5 May was yet another day of inactivity – we spent the day lazing and speculating. The main excitement that day was the arrival at Camp 2 of Göran Kropp, after his extremely valiant attempt to reach the summit despite the high winds of the jet stream.

Göran was an excellent climber, with an ascent of K2 already to his name. He had decided to climb Everest without using any mechanical aids, including aircraft. He had cycled from Sweden via Kathmandu and, more latterly, walked to Base Camp. A Spartan to the end, Göran decided that using the ladders through the Icefall which the rest of us were using was unethical within the rules he had set himself. His route to Camp 1 skirted the left-hand side of the Icefall, passing directly under a number of hanging glaciers. It was a bold, daring alternative to the route the rest of us were taking and, while he pioneered his own route that day, many of us sat in chairs at Base Camp watching his progress and, with a degree of black humour, taking bets on how far he would get before he fell.

Climbing on his own on his summit attempt, Göran got to within a few hundred feet of the top of Everest. One of his interesting public relations ideas was to have an aircraft fly over and film his last few feet to the summit. Yet when Göran arrived in Camp 2 that day, the expression on his face showed more clearly than words what he had recently endured, and it was clear that he had been extremely lucky to survive. Göran would not be so lucky some six years later when he fell to his death while rock-climbing in Washington State in the US.

That same day, the IMAX team of internationally renowned climbers, who were making a film which would be shown on widescreen cinemas around the world, also arrived at Camp 2.

On the Monday the high winds continued, but we were hopeful that a break would come the next day and we checked and prepared our kit. I walked over and chatted with David Breashears, the Everest veteran who was leading the IMAX team. Visiting the other climbers helped to pass the time and in the afternoon the French climber Chantal Mauduit came over to chat. She was attempting to become the first woman to climb Lhotse, which shares the normal route on Everest until the routes split just above Camp 3 on the Lhotse Face. She was a beautiful, delightfully charming character and it was impossible to appreciate that such a charismatic personality would be extinguished within two years.

Most worrying for me was a developing cough which had plagued me earlier in the expedition and had now returned with a vengeance. The 'Khumbu cough', as it is called, affects most Everest climbers sooner or later, as a result of having to breathe cold, dry air over a period of time. It was bad luck that year that I had arrived at the mountain with a chest complaint – even before the effects of altitude added to the problem.

I didn't sleep that night and my cough continued to get worse. I was starting to feel very concerned. I lay there in my sleeping bag and considered my options. If I was going to have any realistic chance of reaching the summit, I would have to return to Base Camp to seek medical help.

Early next morning, I explained this to the others. In the macho sport of mountaineering, backing away from an attempt to reach the summit is a hard decision and I felt that I was letting my partner Jaakko down. Bo and Veikka would be climbing without supplementary oxygen, according to their own plan, which was quite different to the plan Jaakko and I had made, which involved the use of supplementary oxygen.

The others had slept little that night, listening to my constant coughing, and they were very sympathetic. It is hard enough trying to get to sleep at altitude without having to sleep next to, or near, a climber with a rasping cough. It also brings on a degree of hypochondria. Lying there in a sleeping bag, listening to monotonous coughing sounds, it is so easy to imagine oneself coming down with the same complaint – decreasing, or taking away, the chance of reaching the summit.

I quickly packed and left. I travelled light, leaving everything I possibly could at Camp 2. I was now only interested in getting down and back up as soon as possible. My morale was damaged as I trudged down the glacier, despite the light load, with the wretched cough continuing to plague me.

The body lying by the side of the trail just below Camp 2 had been a constant reminder during the previous weeks of the ever lurking dangers. Whoever she or he had been, they were now an anonymous landmark, just one of more than 200 climbers who had died on the mountain since humans first attempted to reach the highest summit on earth. Some have known graves, some have been removed to be disposed of according to their beliefs or religion, and others lie in inaccessible locations, where they will rest forever.

I was forced to stop yet again by a coughing spasm and, as I stood there looking at the anonymous body, I couldn't help but ponder the fragility of life in the mountains. One second climbers can be excited, vibrant, full of life and dreaming of the achievements ahead, but, in an instant, a slip or stumble can cause them to hurtle to the depths below. Climbers often think about the dangers, but as in so many other circumstances in life, it always happens to someone else. Feeling ill and low and looking at that body brought all of the dangers starkly into focus.

It was a bizarre thought, but it occurred to me that lying for eternity on the mountain might be preferable to ending up in the fridge in the German Embassy, en route to a flight home in the hold of an aircraft. The British Embassy didn't, at the time, have a cold box to take bodies, so they used the services of other embassies who could store the bodies of foreign nationals before they were flown home, which usually meant using the German fridge.

Climbers don't have a death wish – they have a life wish. They don't go to Everest to die. Through climbing they are able to experience more of what life has to offer. They fill, as Kipling put it so well, 'the unforgiving minute/With sixty seconds' worth of distance run'. In doing so, climbers sometimes come close to danger, often too close, with disastrous results.

I felt dejected. Everest is not technically difficult, but climbers need to remain healthy if they are to have any chance of getting to the top. Most of us during our time on the mountain become hypochondriacs, concerned that the slightest symptom may turn in to some debilitating disease which will end our dreams of standing on the highest point in the world. On down the Western Cwm I trudged. How different I had felt a few days earlier, when I was going in the opposite direction, full of hope and ambition.

On the way down I met many climbers who were going up to Camp 2, to wait their opportunities to go for the summit. I had got to know many of the climbers from the other teams during our time on the mountain. I had also got to know the Sherpas; during my seventeen years as an officer in the British Army Gurkhas, I had worked in the Nepalese language and it was a unique pleasure to joke and laugh with the Sherpas in their own language. Most of those I met that day were sympathetic to my plight and most feared that they too might have their plans thwarted by illness.

Just below Camp 1, halfway down a steep snow slope, I met Scott Fischer. We swapped banter and I explained that I was descending to get some medicine. Scott said that his chest was also bad, but it would not stop him reaching the summit. I wished him luck and I continued to drag my body downwards, leaving Scott to head upwards, stepping ever nearer to an unfolding tragedy and his death.

It was cold and overcast, which added to my dejection. Dragging one's body downhill, in such a low mental state, is far more difficult than going steeply up in the opposite direction, full of enthusiasm and ambition. It did seem to demonstrate the theory that, when climbing mountains, mental fitness is as important as physical fitness.

Further down I met Mal Duff, who was on his way up with the second summit group, and we discussed what changes would be made to the order in which climbers would now be going to the summit. We agreed to discuss it later that day on the radio, after my medical condition had been assessed at Base Camp.

It took me far longer to get back to Base Camp that day than it did a few days earlier to complete the same journey in the opposite direction. I went straight to see Caroline Mackenzie, Rob Hall's doctor, to seek assistance. She was confident that I could still make the summit that year and she gave me several different medicines, along with orders to rest for at least two days before I went back up the mountain.

Many miles to the east, the weather was not being so kind. Born in the Bay of Bengal, a storm was wreaking havoc. How blissfully unaware we were of what was to take place during the next five days.

Base Camp was virtually empty. During my days of convalescence, the only climber I bumped into was Göran Kropp, who was recovering from his ordeal high on the mountain. He still looked completely wrecked – further evidence of just how much his summit attempt had taken out of him. Ever focused, totally committed, Göran felt that he now knew the route to the summit, and he would be able to climb much faster on his next attempt to reach the top.

Solo attempts to reach the summit of Everest normally take place after other teams have been to the top and cleared the route. It had surprised many that Göran had not waited for others to go first. Kicking a route through deep snow is exhausting and team members normally share the task, but Göran knew what was required. It had been only a week before, while sleeping in a crevasse at Camp 3, that he decided that he was ready, so off he went, heading for the top.

If Göran had not survived, then his decision would have probably been examined and criticised. Such is the difference between survival and death. He had also calculated that if he did not reach the summit, he would still have time to have a second attempt before the end of the season on the mountain. Göran acknowledged that he was lucky – he had been so exhausted that reaching Base Camp on the descent had been an ordeal like no other which he had faced on a mountain. Although I did find Göran's views a little extreme, I admired him greatly.

I didn't meet the Spaniards who had descended from their attempt on the South Pillar route, and who I presumed were also recovering in their tents, somewhere within the maze of camps. The Yugoslavs were busy monitoring the progress of their team members who were planning to go for the summit on 9 May. But even without most of its inhabitants, there was an air of extreme excitement at Base Camp.

One of the big disadvantages of being one of the few native English-speaking climbers left at Base Camp was that I had to talk to a number of visiting trekkers. Having made the effort to walk across the glacier from Kala Patthar, they all seemed to think this entitled them to meet a climber who would tell them what was going on.

More often than not trekkers are not welcome at Base Camp, although they have every right to be there – the trekking permit they have paid for in Kathmandu is valid up to the base of the Icefall. The lack of spaces to pitch tents is the main problem. There just isn't enough space, and the walk in and out from Gorak Shep means that quite often trekkers want to stay at Base Camp, instead of completing the round trip in one day. I had come to Base Camp to rest and recuperate and I could have done without the interruptions caused by the visitors.

The climbers on the mountain had left behind their cooks, camp helpers, Base Camp managers, and Nepalese liaison officers and most of these were monitoring the progress of their fellow team members, almost by the hour, as the time for summit attempts drew near.

Several teams had satellite links to internet sites and they had support staff with them whose sole task was to relay information about what was going on to the outside world. The ability in those days to give news almost as it happened, from such a remote area, was remarkable. It was such an advance from the early days of expeditions to the mountain, when news was carried by Sherpa runners from the Khumbu all the way to Kathmandu. On a previous expedition in the Himalaya I had used the Sherpa runners over a period of a couple of months to buy my house in France.

Emerging technology was a welcome addition which allowed teams on the mountain to keep those waiting back home up-to-date with the news on Everest. My enthusiasm for this 'instant' method of communication would take a knock in the days ahead.

One of the team members who had come to Everest specifically to record events was the British journalist Audrey Salkeld. I have always enjoyed her writing and it made a pleasant excursion to listen to this very knowledgeable lady.

The liaison officers were, as usual, a mixed bunch. It was mandatory for each expedition to have a liaison officer, provided by the Nepalese government and normally selected from volunteers from within the ranks of the civil service. Many of those who end up doing the job are totally unsuited to the role. They frequently come from the low-lying, hot areas of Nepal, and are not familiar with the cold, harsh reality of life at Base Camp. Expeditions have to provide suitable equipment, or pay the liaison officer an allowance to buy the necessary cold weather clothing. The vast majority take the money but turn up at Base Camp with totally unsuitable clothing, having banked their allowance. Quite often the liaison officers will arrive at Base Camp and stay for a few days before claiming illness and scurrying back down the valley to warmer climes. Sometimes they return to Kathmandu, as my liaison officer did when I was leading a team on Annapurna IV in 1992. On that occasion our liaison officer was with us for less than five per cent of the time we spent on the mountain.

The mountaineering section of the Ministry of Tourism does listen to complaints from expedition leaders about liaison officers, and the individual in question is unlikely to be employed in the role again. There have been signs in the years following 1996 that many of those selected for the job are tougher individuals, more so than many of their predecessors. But in 1996, the standard of liaison officer at Base Camp was still not good, which was going to be a factor in the days ahead.

I rested as much as I could. The thicker air of Base Camp seemed to be helping, but I was also taking every item of medicine I could get my hands on. I was desperate to do whatever it took to get back up the mountain. I had forty-eight hours to rest and then I had to return to Camp 2 to join one of our summit groups or, as I thought, I might lose my chance that year to reach the top of the mountain.

Wednesday 8 May passed fairly quietly. I walked down as far as the South African camp to stretch my legs and scrounge a cup of coffee. Deshun Deysel and Ian Woodall's brother Philip were pleasant company to pass time with. What still amazed me was Deshun's continuing loyalty to Ian Woodall, which though commendable, did seem misplaced. She must have become aware by this stage of the expedition that Woodall had never intended to take her on to the mountain.

The South African team of Woodall and O'Dowd, together with the Englishman, Bruce Herrod, were at Camp 2, waiting to shadow the experienced teams when they started out for the summit. Rob Hall in particular had had a very difficult time with Woodall. An argument between the South African and the Adventure Consultants Sherpas a couple of weeks before had resulted in Woodall sending a threatening note to Hall.

I awoke next morning feeling much better, although, retrospectively, my desire to get up the mountain was probably masking any underlying symptoms of my chest complaint. That afternoon thick clouds were forming close to Everest. On the radio I heard that Mal had gone from Camp 2 to the bottom of the Lhotse Face, before turning round as the weather deteriorated. Veikka and Bo had started their summit attempt from Camp 2 and had got to a point on the South Pillar route between Camps 3 and 4, in the gully to the left of the Geneva Spur, before they too had decided to turn round. From Rob Hall's team I heard that Rob and his team had got to Camp 4 on the South Col, but they would probably return tomorrow, to either Camp 3 or Camp 2.

I also heard the more disturbing noise that the Taiwanese climber, Chen Yu-Nan, had died, although details of what had happened were at first a little sketchy. The Taiwanese were regarded by all who saw them climb to be a disaster waiting to happen. They were slow and ill at ease on the mountain. The only surprise was that they had not already had an accident. Watching them in the Icefall, abseiling down a rope, or jumaring up one, their apparent lack of skill was so obvious that it made one really wonder what on earth they were doing on Everest.

Despite grave misgivings about their technical skills, they were a friendly pair. My very limited knowledge of Mandarin always brought a wide smiling response from Chen Yu-Nan whenever I met him on the route, and I felt very sad that he was now lying dead on the mountain.

It transpired that early on the morning of 9 May, Chen left his tent to go to the toilet. He obviously felt safe; he was not wearing crampons, and hadn't bothered to secure himself to the mountain while he was squatting in the snow. It is unclear how he slipped and fell twenty metres down the face into a crevasse, from which he was recovered by Sherpas who carried him back up to Camp 3. His injuries did not at first appear to be that serious, and his companion, Makalu Gau, decided to leave Chen behind and to climb up to Camp 4 for his summit attempt. Some of the IMAX Sherpas, who were returning from a load carry, started to help Chen down the mountain, although they too did not immediately think his condition was serious.

Just before 3 p.m. that afternoon, Chen's condition deteriorated and the IMAX Sherpas radioed this news to Camp 2. Thirty minutes later Chen was dead.

IMAX team members, David Breashears, Ed Viesturs and Robert Schauer, then started up towards Camp 3, in weather which soon deteriorated into a minor blizzard, to bring Chen's body down. It was a noble act, and having placed the body in a sleeping bag, they left Chen on the glacier close to Camp 2, where his body would freeze solid, which would make it easier to drag him through the Western Cwm and the Icefall and down to Base Camp. From there, a helicopter would take him to Kathmandu and onwards to Taiwan.

I didn't sleep well that night. Not because of Chen's death – these things have more impact in retrospect from a distance than they do at the time – I simply didn't sleep because I was excited to have the opportunity of a second attempt at the summit. I didn't feel anything like as debilitated as I had when I arrived down at Base Camp two days before, but I did still have a cough.

I awoke keen and ready to go by 5.30 a.m. I didn't wait to find out how things were going high on the mountain. All I wanted to do was get back up as quickly as possible. I felt strong as I left Base Camp, and I managed to move swiftly up through the Icefall to Camp 1. I stopped briefly and then continued at speed to Camp 2.

With so many people high on the mountain, I only passed a few Sherpas on the way. It was so pleasant to be on the hill again, heading upwards with the hope that I would be on the summit in a few days.

In retrospect, I should not have left Base Camp that day. My illness was bad and, despite Caroline Mackenzie's assurance, I probably knew deep in my heart that I was in no condition to climb. That is easier to conclude now than it was then. At the time, my enthusiasm and drive overrode any signs that I was not up to it.

I arrived at 9.30 a.m. It was my fastest ascent from Base Camp to Camp 2 and, although I had not been a slouch during the expedition, my fellow team members were still surprised by the time. For the remainder of the morning we lazed around, looking up at the mountain, thinking that we were watching a rehearsal of our own summit successes, which would, we hoped, come soon.

None of us that morning considered that things above us were going to go horribly wrong. We knew that Rob and Scott's teams had left the South Col the previous night, and we were now waiting to hear that they had reached the summit. Even the news that some people had turned round and were now heading back to the South Col did not cause anxiety amongst the teams waiting at Camp 2.

It was early afternoon on 10 May 1996 when the first alarm bells started to ring at our camp. From our position we could easily see the Hillary Step, and at about 1 p.m. we could clearly see a small group of a half dozen or so climbers queuing to climb this small notch on the route. It was easy to do a rough calculation, which indicated that by this point their oxygen would be running low. The weather was still good and the knowledge that there were so many guides with the teams above us gave the watchers below a false sense that things would be okay.

Reports followed that climbers were reaching the summit late in the afternoon and these did give rise to greater concern, but this was not the first time that the mountain had been climbed so late in the day and there was still some optimism at Camp 2 that all would be well.

The weather from our position still looked okay. We could not, of course, see the clouds rolling in from the east, as the climbers could from their various positions between the summit and the South Col.

At about 4 p.m. the weather high on the mountain suddenly deteriorated. The winds increased to about 120 kilometres per hour and it started to snow. My most vivid memory is of the darkness which covered the mountain long before the sun set. From where we were the summit ridge looked black. At last the alarm bells at Camp 2 rang loud and clear. Small groups formed with everyone looking upwards, hoping and praying that things would be okay.

Messages from Base Camp gave us little clue of exactly what was going on above us. With so many climbers on the mountain there was no one at Base Camp to relay meaningful information to us at the higher camp. If anything, what little information was reaching us was just further confusing our picture of what was going on.

And then, at about 6 p.m., we heard the most alarming news – Rob Hall was still near the summit with his client Doug Hansen, who was in a bad condition. A short time later we learned that Doug's condition was very serious and we sensed that he would have difficulty surviving the night – but Rob could survive if he left Doug, and in such appalling conditions he had to do this soon.

What Rob did that night was honourable and brave, and it ultimately cost him his life. It was not possible to get Doug down the mountain and yet Rob decided to stay with him so that he would not die alone. When Rob made these decisions, he was probably still capable of clear thought and could have survived – he knew the risks, and he knew the consequences – it was an extremely brave act.

Those below all agreed on what Rob had to do. We willed him to leave Doug and to save his own life. It was very clear that there was not much time for Rob to do this before he too would have little chance of getting back down to safety.

There was little sleep, if any, at camp that night. The storm continued to batter the mountain all through the hours of darkness. In the tents it was impossible not to think of just how bad it would be for those still outside the tents at the South Col. At this stage we thought this was only Rob and Doug.

8

DEATH IS A STONE'S THROW AWAY

The decision by Rob and Scott to go for the summit on 10 May had been made some time in advance, because Rob had reached the top on four previous occasions around this date (10 May 1990, 12 May 1992, 10 May 1993 and 9 May 1994) and he had assumed that the weather would again be suitable during this period. They had also asked other teams to stay clear of the route on that day.

There was little science involved in making the decision so far in advance. It had more to do with luck. It was also in conflict with Rob Hall's advice to others on the mountain that they should wait for the right conditions, whenever that might be. He was fond of saying that death on Everest was often a result of 'summit fever', the disease which results from climbers becoming impatient and going for the summit before they are ready, or when the weather is not suitable, or both. It is a 'disease' which has resulted in many deaths over the years.

Rob and Scott's teams left Camp 2 on 8 May to make the climb up the steep Lhotse Face to Camp 3, which was located in a crevassed area in the centre of the face. The face was steep and ice-covered, but by early May a series of footsteps had formed, made by the passage of climbers up to camps 3 and 4.

Behind the two guided teams came the South Africans and the Taiwanese. It is unclear whether or not the Taiwanese were simply reneging on an agreement made with Hall not to climb that day, but Woodall, the South African team leader, had always had a difficult relationship with Hall and it is unlikely, in my opinion, that he had agreed not to move according to the wishes of the New Zealander.

Woodall was inexperienced as a high-altitude climber, having never climbed high before on a Himalayan giant. All the other teams had been asked not to make a summit attempt at the same time as Rob and Scott's groups. It was not surprising, however, that Woodall ignored this request, given that with his lack of high altitude climbing experience it made sense for him to follow teams led by two of the most experienced leaders on Everest. It was presumably the same reason that the Taiwanese team, which also lacked Himalayan experience, decided to follow behind Rob and Scott. They all made Camp 3 safely, although guide Andy Harris was hit by a stone just before the teams reached the tents.

Nowadays most teams use oxygen on a slow flow rate at Camp 3 to give their members a better night's sleep. What is left in the cylinders is used next day on the climb up to the South Col.

There is a misapprehension about using oxygen on mountains. Generally, climbers are described as climbing with or without oxygen. Of course, this is rubbish, everyone climbs with oxygen, as otherwise they would die. More accurately, some climbers use extra, or supplementary, oxygen. The effect on the body depends on the flow rate from the cylinder to the mask, but supplementary oxygen can help the body perform as it would if the climber was some thousand metres lower down the mountain without the supplementary oxygen. The body gets some assistance but the strain of climbing at altitude is only reduced by a relatively small amount.

It was early the following morning, on 9 May, that the Taiwanese climber Chen Yu-Nan had his accident while going to the toilet at Camp 3 where he slipped and fell some twenty metres, landing in a crevasse lower down the face.

The climb that day took the climbers further up the Lhotse Face, past the Yellow Band, and diagonally up and across to Camp 4 at the South Col. There they would rest until almost midnight, when they would start their climb to the summit. There was already some concern, as the climbers left Camp 3, that there were too many of them moving on the route at the same time.

As the leading climbers started to reach the South Col, they could see the Yugoslavian team high on the south-east ridge, attempting to become the first team that year to summit. The Yugoslavs had generally kept to themselves on the mountain. They were a large team, with seemingly endless funding. They regularly used the satellite phone owned by the Danish members of our team. The phone cost $10 per minute to use and it was not uncommon for the Yugoslavs to run up a daily bill of several hundred US dollars.

Their team leader was in his sixties and appeared to be more of an academic than a mountaineer. He had remained at Base Camp until he became seriously ill and had to be evacuated to a hospital in Kathmandu. It was never clear, after his departure, who had taken over from him as leader of the expedition.

The Yugoslavs were, without a doubt, a hard and tough bunch, and despite strong winds high on the mountain they did well that day to get as high as they did, but eventually they admitted defeat and started to descend. They did not reach the South Col until about 11 p.m. that night, having descended for much of the day in foul weather.

Down on the Lhotse Face the first death of the season had already occurred. Chen Yu-Nan's condition had deteriorated and he died shortly afterwards. His partner, Makalu Gau, was by this time in his wind-blown tent at the South Col. On hearing the shocking news about Chen's death, which was radioed to him by IMAX team leader David Breashears, Makalu concluded that his summit attempt was now over – a decision which he later changed, almost costing him his life.

The weather on the South Col was bleak. The wind was blowing hard and conditions worsened as the day progressed. It is tough to imagine what it was like higher up, as the Yugoslavs made their way down after failing in their bid to reach the top.

It is surprising, given the worsening weather conditions, that there were no major problems with any of the teams that day as they made their way to the South Col. The South African team in particular became split up and arrived at the col much later than the others.

The weather was fickle that night. If the storm had continued, it is likely that everyone would have retreated down the mountain the following day to safety. However, at about 7 p.m. the weather suddenly cleared and a window of opportunity appeared. Rob and Scott then made the ultimately fateful decision to go for the summit that night. If only the wind had kept blowing for a little bit longer, things may have turned out differently.

Just before midnight, most teams, including the remaining Taiwanese climber Makalu Gau, who had by then decided, despite the death of his climbing partner, to attempt to reach the summit, assembled outside their tents to start the final push to the top. Fortunately, the South Africans had such a hard time just getting to the South Col that they decided not to try to get to the summit, one of the few things that went right that night. The weather was fairly clear and calm, but it didn't take long before some climbers started to have doubts and returned to the South Col.

One of Rob Hall's team members, Doug Hansen, who had been high on Everest the previous year, also wanted to turn around, but Rob Hall had a discussion with him and Doug kept going.

As the climbers ascended they inevitably began to spread out. Those at the front had to regularly stop to allow those at the back to catch up. This does seem to have been an odd tactic, given the fact that there were six guides between the two main groups. Some of the stops were as long as ninety minutes and this appears to have caused a degree of frustration amongst the fitter, faster climbers.

Guiding large commercial groups at altitude was still in its relative infancy in 1996. There were two options open to the teams on the mountain that day. One was to use the guides to 'herd' their clients up to the summit, and the other was to allocate guides to smaller groups of similarly fit climbers, who could have then moved at their own speed. The leaders decided on the herding option.

If the fitter climbers had been able to move at their own speed that day there would probably have been a process of natural selection. The front runners could have summited early, within an acceptable time frame, and it would have become obvious that those who were at the back of the line were not going to get safely to the top and back. What, in fact, happened was that the climbers, particularly in Rob Hall's team, were forced to stay together, which held back the faster climbers. Everyone was now moving at a slow, dangerous pace. It inevitably meant there would be bunching at the choke points.

Dawn came at 5.30 a.m. as some climbers waited for ninety minutes at a feature called the Balcony for the slower climbers to catch up. Inevitably, the control and the resultant slow pace caused clients, guides and Sherpas to become increasingly frustrated. A further problem was caused by the lack of fixed rope. It is unclear what the plan actually was that day for the fixing of rope, but whatever it was, it wasn't working, and further hold-ups occurred as new plans were debated.

The Spanish pair and Göran Kropp had been high, but they had not used any fixed ropes. The only other team who had been high enough that year to fix ropes had been the Yugoslavs, but they had over-fixed the route closer to the South Col and there were still long sections higher up which had not been fixed, because the Yugoslavs had run out of rope.

By late morning, some of the clients had worked out that they would not reach the summit within the safe time frame that had been discussed lower on the mountain. Sensibly, three of Rob's team, Stuart Hutchison, John Taske and Lou Kasischke, turned round and, accompanied by two Sherpas, returned to the South Col.

Oddly that day there were guides and Sherpas who were not using supplementary oxygen. These two types of professional climbers were being employed to take clients to the summit and were not there for their own benefit, but for the benefit of those who had paid, in this case, large sums of money to use their services. They should have taken all precautions to make sure that they could perform as well as possible, as would be expected by the clients, particularly, if things went wrong. Climbing without supplementary oxygen meant that there was a limited amount of time that they could spend above the South Col and, given the speed that the groups were moving at, for those without supplementary oxygen, time was quickly running out.

In 1996 it was normal practice to use three cylinders of oxygen on a summit attempt from the South Col – an arrangement which provided a sensible safety margin. Client climbers carry two cylinders, and their third cylinder is carried by their Sherpas and cached at the South Summit. Including their own oxygen cylinders, the Sherpas carry four and the clients carry two. The first cylinder carried by the climber lasts as far as the South Summit, the second lasts from there to the summit and back, and the third cylinder, the one carried by the Sherpas and cached at the South Summit, should enable the climber to make it safely back to the South Col. However, at the speed the climbers were moving, the safety margin provided by using three cylinders was fast disappearing.

The first climbers reached the summit at about 1 p.m., and shortly after the early signs appeared that the weather was deteriorating. The remaining climbers who reached the summit that day arrived over the next three hours. The early arrivals now started to make their way back down, but the initial problem facing them was the bottleneck caused by the main group, still climbing upwards.

Oxygen was fast running out and any safety margins were fast disappearing. Irrespective of the deteriorating weather, there was already a high probability, given how late it already was, that something was going to go horribly wrong.

The weather itself was also having an impact – as the storm moved in the air pressure became lower, which further reduced the amount of oxygen that the climbers were breathing in from the outside air. Provided their oxygen systems were still working, they were getting the same whiff of oxygen from their cylinders, but given they were getting less from outside, the overall effect meant that they were increasingly breathing in less oxygen.

It was from this point on that events high on the mountain became less clear. A phenomenon was occurring on Everest which can be compared to what is so aptly called in the army 'the fog of war'. Even the apparently fastest and fittest climbers who had reached the summit at the head of the ascending climbers were now starting to have problems, and before some of them arrived back at the South Summit to collect their third cylinders, the oxygen in their second cylinders had started to run out.

Of the two leaders, Rob reached the summit shortly after 2 p.m., where he waited for two hours until Doug Hansen arrived. Scott was obviously ill and unable to lead as he normally did. He was coming up very slowly and arrived at the summit at about 3.40 p.m. There can be little doubt, from the various descriptions, that Scott was suffering from the complaint which he had described to me when I talked to him in the Icefall three days before.

The third senior guide that day, the Russian Anatoli Boukreev, had not used supplementary oxygen and he had already returned on his own to the South Col. In effect, half of the guides, including the two leaders, were now either not in a position to help their clients, or were quickly approaching that state.

By mid-afternoon the weather had taken a definite turn for the worst. It had started to snow heavily and the clouds were now covering the mountain causing a condition known as 'white-out'. Quite simply, white-out describes the situation where, in thick cloud, wherever you look everything appears white. It is impossible to know what exists a metre in front of you; it could be anything, including of course on Everest, a sheer drop.

In 1976 I had been climbing a new route in the Canadian Rockies. During the descent off the mountain, the weather deteriorated and my partner and I were caught in a white-out in an area with sheer drops all around us. It was getting cold and dark and without being able to find any shelter we were forced to keep moving. We made large snowballs, which we rolled a few inches in front of us; if one disappeared we changed direction. It had been extremely touch and go and we gradually found our way out of danger. But we had been at relatively low altitude and it was nothing compared to the dangers being faced high on Everest as the afternoon of 10 May 1996 wore on.

Whatever the rights and wrongs, Rob Hall had told one of his climbers, Beck Weathers, to wait at the Balcony until Rob returned from the summit to escort Beck back down to the South Col. Beck remained there for over ten hours, during which time at least three fellow team members, two Sherpas, and one guide passed him on their way back down the mountain before he accompanied one of the Adventure Consultants guides back to Camp 4. Even if Rob had got to the summit and back in a reasonable time, Beck would still have spent some hours sitting and waiting at over 8,000 metres.

It was probably an oversight by Rob that he didn't ask his three clients and two Sherpas to collect Beck on their way down. But why didn't Anatoli take Beck down when he had returned earlier from the summit? He may not have been in the same team, but he was a guide who knew that it would be some time before Rob returned to escort Beck to safety.

The weather continued to deteriorate and by early evening a fully developed storm was hitting the mountain. The majority of climbers were still high on the mountain, still hours from the safety of the South Col.

Those below at Camp 2 and Base Camp, who had been monitoring the progress of Rob and Scott's teams, were by now starting to become alarmed. It was, however, difficult for the watchers to gain an accurate picture of events on the mountain, a problem that would get worse as the night progressed. Communications were breaking down as radios started to malfunction and batteries ran out. Another 'fog of war' factor.

From below at Camp 2, the weather on the south-east ridge looked horrific and it was easy to imagine what was happening to anyone who was stuck in such ferocious conditions. Modern climbing clothes can only give a certain amount of protection and, from what we could see from the Western Cwm, taking into account the ferocity of the weather and the position of the climbers who were still high on the mountain, the design limitations of their clothing was going to be severely tested.

The conditions were so bad that when the survivors reached the South Col they were still not out of danger. In the near zero visibility, it was becoming extremely difficult to find the tents. The South Col measures about 400 by 200 metres. It is a flat, virtually featureless area, which even in normal conditions is subject to high winds being forced through the gap in which the col sits, between Everest on one side, and the world's fourth highest mountain, Lhotse, on the other. Some climbers, after arriving at the col, spent over four hours searching for their tents in the fierce conditions.

During the day, while the teams were moving up to the summit, several other climbers arrived at the South Col. These teams had intended to climb to the summit one day after Rob and Scott's teams and hoped to benefit from the tracks through the deep snow which the two teams would have carved.

As well as the South Africans and the lone French climber Thierry Renard, members of Henry Todd's Himalayan Guides commercial expedition had arrived, although Henry had remained at Camp 2. Conditions were so bad on the South Col that it was a battle for survival for everyone, inside and outside the tents.

On the other side of the mountain, conditions were just as bad. During the pre-monsoon season from the end of March into May, and the post monsoon season from August to October, teams attempt to climb Everest from both the Tibetan and Nepalese sides of the mountain. Permits for the Chinese side were cheaper at the time, and cost $3,000 per team with no limit on the number of climbers who could be put on the permit. An increasing number of climbers are attracted to the lower costs of climbing on the Tibetan side, even though the success rate is traditionally higher on the Nepalese side of the mountain.

Late in the afternoon of 10 May, three Indian climbers had reached, from the northern side of the mountain, what they thought was the summit. They were actually still a significant distance from the top, but they were unaware of this. The news of their apparent success was relayed from their Base Camp to Delhi. The three climbers never made it back to their top camp.

Just after 1.30 p.m. on 11 May, three Japanese climbers left their top camp to climb to the summit. Given the weather conditions prevailing at the time, this would appear to have been a suicidal attempt to reach the top of the world. Certainly on the Nepalese side the storm was raging with all its fury. Perhaps conditions were not quite so bad on the northern side, but in relative terms the weather must still have been extreme.

What happened during the Japanese climbers' summit push is not absolutely clear and it has been the subject of a great deal of subsequent debate. The most accusatory view suggests that the Japanese passed by the Indians, who were still alive, without offering any help whatsoever, even though at least one of the Indians was lying frozen in the snow begging for assistance.

Amazingly, the Japanese climbers reached the summit despite the horrendous weather conditions. On their return, they again encountered the Indians, who were dead by this stage.

Back in the raging storm on the Nepalese side of Everest there were attempts by some climbers on the South Col that night to go out into the teeth of the storm to search for those who were still missing, or to make noises which hopefully would lead the missing climbers to the relative safety of the tents. Most notable among those who left their tents that night were the guide Anatoli Boukreev, to whom several climbers owe their lives, and the Canadian doctor Stuart Hutchison.

I had got to know Stuart on the walk in. He was an extremely intelligent and capable man for whom I have the greatest respect. Next day he was to become a vital link between the rescuers below and the South Col.

The last climbers to get to their tents that night arrived at about 4.30 a.m. on the morning of 11 May. By this time they had been above the South Col for almost thirty hours, they had been without supplementary oxygen for around ten hours and they had been in the teeth of a storm for up to fourteen hours. It is surprising that more climbers did not perish that day.

At 5.30 a.m. on 11 May we were all up and dressed, standing outside our tents gazing up at the storm raging above us. It was clear to us at Camp 2 that something terrible had happened. The priority now was to find out what had happened and to then make plans to make sure that the situation didn't get any worse.

It was only a short time later that we learned more about the full extent of the disaster. Rob was still just below the summit with Doug Hansen, who, it was thought, had already died, but this was not absolutely clear. Below Rob, a further twenty-one climbers were unaccounted for. Shortly afterwards we heard that several climbers had made it back to the South Col, but some were in a critical condition. At least three climbers were missing and, we were told, another two bodies had been found.

The situation continued to remain far from clear. Those left at Base Camp were mainly volunteers who had come to Everest not to climb but to help with administration and logistics, and they were not experienced in dealing with disaster situations. To compound the problem, they had worked under enormous pressure throughout the night and by the next morning some were close to breaking point.

Camp 2 that day was fortunately well stocked with experience. There were many professional, semi-professional and very experienced amateur climbers assembled there ready to make their summit attempts. Above were the two teams on the mountain with a large number of commercial clients, the remaining Taiwanese climber, the inexperienced South African team and members of Henry Todd's expedition who had reached the South Col the day before, although Henry himself was still with us at Camp 2. The one thing we did have was the right people in the right place to facilitate any rescue.

The weak link was at Base Camp. It was thought that we had no one there who could give the necessary support and co-ordination which was going to be needed. An informal rescue committee was formed which included David Breashears, Mal Duff and Henry Todd, and I was asked to go down to Base Camp to co-ordinate the support that was required. I was no more experienced than many at Camp 2 that day, but I did uniquely speak Nepalese which we thought would be an important asset.

I quickly packed, but far from being buoyant and excited, as I had been the day before, I now felt depressed and mentally exhausted. I knew that by going down so quickly after I had returned from my recuperative period at Base Camp, my ambitions to climb Everest in 1996 were finished. This didn't seem to bother me in the slightest, when saving further lives was the common mission of all of us on Everest that morning, but it had a sub-conscious effect and I felt very tired.

Mal sent me a Sherpa to help me carry my gear off the mountain, and we set off to get to Base Camp as quickly as possible. Looking back up, the weather above seemed clearer but the wind still howled across the mountain.

I have rarely felt so tired as I did descending Everest that morning. Despite knowing how important it was for me to get to Base Camp as quickly as possible, I found myself having to take frequent rests. These stops seemed to have no effect and I had to force myself onwards. Most worryingly I started to vomit, which alarmed the Sherpa who was accompanying me.

The Western Cwm passed and at last I was prevented by the western shoulder of Everest from looking back up at the South Col. I descended through the Icefall, my mind really unaware of the passing features. All I could think about was getting as far as I could before I had to collapse again and vomit in the snow. It took me twice as long to return downhill to Base Camp as it had to make the uphill journey the day before.

At last I stumbled into Base Camp. Gone was the sense of excitement which had pervaded the atmosphere only a short time before. It had been replaced everywhere by a deep gloom. It was difficult to imagine how on earth I was going to become dynamic enough to turn this sense of complete depression into an organisation that was going to be able to provide the support which I knew was desperately needed by those above.

The one light in the gloom was the arrival of Guy Cotter, a New Zealand mountain guide and employee of Adventure Consultants who had been leading a team on neighbouring Pumori. Guy knew the details of Rob's summit attempt, which he had regularly monitored by tuning in to Rob's radio frequency to follow his friend's progress on the mountain. When Guy heard that things were going wrong he rushed from Pumori to Everest to give whatever assistance he could.

The one thing that I have learned from my years in the army, and particularly from my time working in war-torn Yugoslavia, is that things will only get more complicated if you try and sort a bad situation out with a fogged mind. I was feeling exhausted and ill and if I was going to do the job I had been sent down to do, then rest was vital. In any case the situation on the mountain was still very confused and it was not going to be possible to organise the appropriate support until the situation we faced became clearer. I talked briefly to Guy and the head Nepalese liaison officer, and I scheduled a meeting at which I wanted all liaison officers and a representative from all of the teams on the mountain to attend.

I then went to my tent and attempted to close my eyes for two hours.

9

LEAVING THE DEAD –
SORTING OUT THE LIVING

Out of the Gloom,
A voice said unto me,
'Smile and be happy,
Things could get worse',
And behold, things did get worse!
– Source unknown

I tried to sleep – I desperately wanted to feel more capable to deal with the tasks which lay ahead. Despite my exhaustion, my mind continued to turn over the options which needed to be considered. The short, deep, refuelling, unconscious state which I desperately sought eluded me. At last I gave up trying to sleep and I hauled myself over to the Adventure Consultants' dining tent which would be our rescue headquarters during the days ahead.

One of the perverse ironies of the situation was that the extra money paid by the Adventure Consultants clients was going to pay dividends which they could never have dreamed of when they had booked to climb Everest. Their large and comfortable dining tent had seating down either side and along the end opposite to the entrance to the tent. It made an ideal venue in which to hold the co-ordination meetings which were going to become a twice-daily feature over the next seventy-two hours. The dining tent was also located adjacent to the communications tent, which housed their excellent radio equipment, which would keep us in contact with the mountain and the outside world. It was already being ably manned around the clock by Helen Wilton, Rob Hall's Base Camp manager, and other members of the Adventure Consultants Base Camp support staff.

Much has been said about the communications, or more accurately the lack of communications, during the early stages of the developing tragedy. The critical comment was to some extent based on a seeming unwillingness by the South African team at the South Col to let some of the members of Rob Hall's team have access to Ian Woodall's radio.

Both Adventure Consultants and the South Africans had excellent, and similar, communications equipment at Base Camp, with which they were in daily contact with New Zealand and South Africa via a satellite over the Indian Ocean. They also had powerful radios for use on the mountain, but these systems were dependent on line of sight and obstacles such as the lip at the top of the Icefall had a degrading effect on the quality of radio transmissions.

Up on the mountain, when the Adventure Consultants team's radio batteries started to run out, the most efficient means of communicating with the South Col was via the South Africans' radio. By mid-morning on 11 May, the very experienced climbers Pete Athans and Todd Burleson had reached the South Col to give whatever assistance was needed and from then on communications were significantly improved.

Besides the remnants of the Adventure Consultants and Mountain Madness teams and the South Africans, the Himalayan Guides climbers were also on the South Col on the morning of 11 May, having climbed up from Camp 3 the day before, en route to their own summit attempt.

Ian Woodall was not popular amongst other climbers on Everest, due mainly to his often aggressive manner towards other team leaders, in particular Rob Hall, but I feel that he was, on occasion, used as an easy scapegoat when things went wrong. He was a team leader responsible for those whom he was leading, in conditions which were still extreme. His first responsibility was to his team and at that time he had to make sure that they would be safe – his radio was first and foremost for the use of

1   At Mirbat, in Oman, July 1973.
2   With Peter Boardman (*right*) in Hong Kong, 1981.
3   660 Squadron, Army Air Corps, Hong Kong, 1982. I am piloting 'Bravo' at the bottom of the stack.
4   L–R: Everest (8,848 metres), Lhotse (8,516 metres) and Nuptse (7,861 metres), taken from the shoulder
    of Pumori (7,161 metres).   *Photo: Mal Duff.*

5

5   Crossing one of the bridges in the Icefall.
6   Climbing a cliff in the Icefall, 1996.

7   The ever-lurking possibility of a collapse in the Icefall, 1996.
8   Ginge Fullen is carried into Base Camp, 20 April 1996.
9   Göran Kropp at Camp 2, May 1996. He was killed in 2002 while rock climbing in the US.
10 Chantal Mauduit, on her way to climbing Lhotse in 1996. She was to die just two years later
     on Dhaulagiri (8,167 metres).

11 Makalu Gau arrives in Base Camp having been plucked by helicopter from Camp 1.
12 Makalu Gau waits at Base Camp while the helicopter makes a second flight up to Camp 1 to collect Beck Weathers.
13 The helicopter, piloted by Colonel Madan Chhetri, delivers Beck Weathers to Base Camp.
14 With our Base Camp Manager Mick Burns (*left*), and the 'Icefall Doctors' (*centre*), 1997.
15 Escorting the body of Nima Rinzi, 8 May 1997.
16 Mal Duff at Base Camp, April 1997.

17 The magnificence of the Western Cwm, as seen from Camp 1.
18 The Khumbu Icefall.
19 The Western Cwm: Camp 2 is located on the left, under the South-West Face,
and Camp 3 is perched in the centre, in the crevasses on the steep face of Lhotse.

20 Sherpas appearing at Camp 3, 12 May 1999. Camp 2 can be
    seen far below in the middle of the left-hand side of the photo.
21 Camp 2 in the Western Cwm.
22 The South Col, 12 May 1999.

23 The view from the South Col up to the South Summit. The Balcony is the prominent feature
   in the centre of the right-hand ridge.
24 The view from the South Summit looking up the knife-edge ridge to the Hillary Step.
25 On the summit of Everest, 13 May 1999. On my left, with the Greek flag, is Constantine Niarchos.
26 The highest protest in the world – attempting to save my local hospital, on the summit
   of Everest, 13 May 1999.

25

26

27 With Pertemba Sherpa and Sir Chris Bonington at a charity event in 2010.
28 Dining with Sir Edmund Hillary in Kathmandu in 2007.

his team. However, I have no doubt that a more co-operative approach to others involved in the rescue would have been appreciated.

The Adventure Consultants radios were by this stage running out of batteries – why didn't they have sufficient spares? Even if things had not gone badly wrong, the teams who had gone to the summit on 10 May would have expected to be on the mountain until at least as late as 12 May, given the amount of time it takes to descend to Base Camp. They would have needed spare batteries to keep communications going throughout that period.

The obvious solution was for Woodall, with his radio, to go out on to the South Col to assess what was happening and then to act as a relay station between Base Camp and the teams high on the mountain. To some extent, this is what Woodall actually did, but by this time he was so mistrusted by all those on the mountain that any information he sent was never fully accepted. What we needed at Base Camp was a reliable and experienced source of information, and Pete and Todd provided this from the moment they arrived at the South Col on the morning of 11 May.

My first task before the first co-ordination meeting at Base Camp on the afternoon of 11 May was to talk to Guy Cotter and Caroline Mackenzie in order to update myself on what was happening and to discuss what needed to be done.

I had met Caroline on the walk in. She was an extremely intelligent individual who had the most pleasant of personalities. It would soon transpire that she was excellent in a crisis situation and she proved to be a tremendous asset during the next seventy-two hours. She was always cool and calm, even when she was handling the most stressful of situations. She was obviously on occasions moved and upset – she was a very close friend of some of those involved and she had to relay some terrible news – but it never for one second stopped Caroline doing a most remarkable and professional job.

I asked Caroline to contact climbers who could give first-hand confirmation about the deaths on or above the South Col. In all the confusion,

I didn't want us to be working on second- or third-hand information. In the cases of Yasuko Namba and Beck Weathers, for example, I wanted to have confirmation that they were dead from whoever had gone over to check their bodies and not via the South Africans who had heard the news from someone else.

We were told that Beck and Yasuko were definitely dead, although we were soon to discover that this was certainly not the case with Beck. We were also told that Andy Harris had been close to the South Col when he was last seen and it was thought that he had fallen down the Lhotse Face. We checked with Camp 2, who had searched the face with binoculars, but they had been unable to see any sign of a body. It was assumed that he had probably fallen to the bottom of the face, which was not visible from Camp 2.

Not long after Caroline received the 'confirmation' about the dead climbers, we received the news that Beck was in fact alive at the South Col, but his condition was very grave and he was not expected to survive.

Guy Cotter is a tough, capable, professional New Zealand climbing guide, who had reached the summit of Everest in 1992 when he had been a member of a team led by Rob Hall. He had also guided on Everest for Rob in 1995. His intelligence and pragmatic approach to problems would soon become extremely useful and I found him an ideal partner to work with in a crisis. Guy later described our working relationship:

All the while people on the mountain were mobilising to assist on the col. Mike Trueman, who was on Mal Duff's team, had a military background and did a great job in formalising the rescue by looking at the overall picture. Numbers missing, status of survivors, supplies available, rescuers movements etc. Mike facilitated the meeting we had and everybody contributed. I was amazed at how willing and supportive everybody was even though that assistance potentially spelt the failure of their own expeditions through exhausting all of their resources.

From his expedition on Pumori, Guy had spoken to Rob shortly after the latter reached the summit. At that stage there appeared to be no significant cause for concern, although Guy would have known that time was moving on.

Just before 5 p.m. on 10 May, Guy heard Rob telling Base Camp that Doug was now out of oxygen and unable to move. Guy came on the radio and urged Rob to descend to the South Summit where spare oxygen would be available. Rob said he could move but Doug Hansen could not. It was the start of a very brave and selfless act on Rob's part.

During the next hour Guy twice talked to Rob, who it appeared was, by this time, somewhere near the Hillary Step. He continued to encourage Rob to leave Doug and make his own way down the mountain.

During the night, just before 3 a.m. on 11 May, Guy heard Rob on the radio, seemingly urging Doug to move. When Hall called just before 5 a.m., apparently from the South Summit, he said that Doug was no longer with him. During this call, which was received by Caroline Mackenzie at the Adventure Consultants Base Camp, Rob indicated that he was having great difficulties moving. He also referred to 'Harold', the nickname of Andy Harris. Rob gave the impression that Andy had been with him at some stage during the night, but this was contrary to information which had previously been received at Base Camp from other members of Rob's team on the South Col. It was, therefore, assumed by those below that Rob was hallucinating.

Shortly after 5 a.m., Rob's wife, Jan Arnold, who was at home in Christchurch, New Zealand, expecting their first child, was linked through to Rob. Jan was a doctor and she had reached the summit of Everest with Rob in 1993. She knew exactly how bad a situation Rob was in. She also knew both the medical problems and the physical problems facing Rob if he was going to survive.

At 6 a.m. Guy again talked to Rob. It was becoming clear that by this stage he was in a very bad way – for those listening on the radio it was extremely moving and upsetting. It was an Apollo 13 situation – disaster seemed inevitable and those listening could only pray and hope for a miracle.

The winds continued to howl as the morning of 11 May dawned at the South Col, although the visibility had somewhat improved.

Before the arrival of Pete Athans and Todd Burleson at the South Col, the situation was far from clear, largely due to poor communications and a lack of centralised control. All of the expeditions were still working on different radio frequencies and messages had to be relayed by changing frequency, or someone had to be sent from one team to another to let the others know what was going on. This was happening at the South Col, Camp 2 and Base Camp. This could mean that a message from the South Col had to be relayed through the South Africans to their Base Camp, then written down and taken by hand to the IMAX camp, from where it was relayed to their team at Camp 2.

Add to this the fact that batteries were starting to run out, the weather was less than perfect, people were getting tired and there was still, as the day dawned on the morning of 11 May, no one at Base Camp with the necessary experience to co-ordinate a problem like this, and you had a recipe for continuing chaos and for further disaster.

At the South Col on the morning of 11 May there were a number of categories of climber. There were (as we thought at that time) the dead or the dying: Beck and Yasuko. There were the exhausted survivors: the remaining members of Rob's and Scott's teams. There were those who had not gone for the summit on the night of 9–10 May: the South Africans and the lone French climber. And there were the climbers who had arrived at the South Col late the previous day: the members of the Himalayan Guides team.

At dawn on 11 May, we were aware at Camp 2 that above us we had a number of cases of minor frostbite, a large number suffering from exhaustion and a case or two of snow blindness. We knew there had been deaths but beyond that we had no clear picture with which to work.

At 8 a.m. Stuart Hutchison left his tent on the South Col, together with some Sherpas, and walked the short distance to where he knew Beck and Yasuko were lying in the snow. Stuart was absolutely exhausted, having for much of the night tried so hard to guide his fellow team members back to safety, yet would not give up. On reaching the two climbers in the snow, Stuart found that in his opinion they were very close to death.

Doctors have to make life and death decisions every day, but these are normally made in the sterile confines of hospitals, with the full range of modern technology available to assist in the decision-making process. It wasn't a case that day of Stuart making the wrong decision – he didn't. What he made was, for him, the right decision in the circumstances that were prevailing.

Years before, I had made a life and death decision which still haunts me. I had been flying a helicopter along the river which separates Hong Kong from China, while looking for illegal immigrants. The helicopter was small, with two seats in the front and no side doors and nothing in the back. On one side, strapped in, but sitting on the floor, was my aircrewman, and on the other side was a young Royal Navy officer who had volunteered to come on patrol that day. Suddenly I got a message to fly to a position where one of our infantry patrols had seen a young Chinese girl having problems in the river. When I got there she had already been hauled out of the river and was lying on the bank. The patrol handed her to the naval officer. Although by turning my head I could just see, I couldn't from where I sat see whether she was alive or not. I asked the naval officer on our headset radio what her condition was, and he said that he thought she was dead.

I flew the short distance to the grass landing pad where we sometimes dropped off dead bodies, and the girl was laid on the grass. As we lifted off I looked down and the thought struck me that she could still be alive, but I was being summoned to another incident where the helicopter was needed. I still occasionally think of that girl – even with hindsight she was still dead in my opinion – but my regret is that I wasn't able to confirm her death.

While I had not been qualified to make my decision, Stuart was; weighing up the advantages and disadvantages of the situation, and based on his professional knowledge, Stuart decided to leave Beck and Yasuko where they were. Stuart played a significant role in events at the South Col and I believe he deserved far more recognition than he subsequently received.

When Stuart got back to his tent, he discussed his decision with other members of the Adventure Consultants team. They agreed with Stuart's view and the decision was made to leave Beck and Yasuko where they lay, close to the edge of the Kangshung Face.

Given the exhausted state of most of the survivors at the South Col, why didn't Woodall, who had spent the night in his tent, go and bring Beck and Yasuko into the tents? He later admitted that he was told as early as 6 a.m. that morning that the two climbers were lying in the snow relatively close to the South Africans' tents. But despite knowing that Beck and Yasuko were not far away, Woodall did not go and see what could be done. This does seem to be odd, but the same question could be asked of the other climbers who had arrived at the col the previous day – why did they not go and see what could be done?

Another criticism of Ian Woodall's behaviour at the South Col came from the IMAX leader, David Breashears, who radioed Woodall to ask him if he would loan a radio to the survivors at the South Col to aid communications. As David subsequently described it, the South Africans were lying in their sleeping bags and when he asked for the radio to be loaned, even though the South Africans were 'only a few feet away from where survivors of the storm lay huddled and crying, the leader, Ian Woodall, refused'.

Not long after Stuart's discussion with his other team members, Neal Beidleman assembled the remaining members of the Mountain Madness team and led them down the mountain.

Some time before 9 a.m., it appeared that Rob had managed to clear the ice from his mask and it was hoped that at last he was again breathing supplementary oxygen, but by this time his condition was grave. His friends below continued to send him messages of encouragement.

At 9.30 a.m. two Sherpas from Rob's team, Ang Dorje and Lhakpa Chhiri, left the South Col carrying spare oxygen and hot drinks, to attempt to climb up to rescue their expedition leader. Both climbers had reached the summit the day before and, despite being exhausted, were now attempting a climb of almost ten hours to reach Rob. In spite of ferocious winds, the two Sherpas valiantly continued upwards. Given what had happened the day before, the further they got from the South Col the more precarious their own situation become.

Later that day, some 250 metres below where their expedition leader was thought to be, and in the face of extreme cold and winds, the two Sherpas were forced to give up. This most valiant effort, by two brave men to save another brave person, was the last chance Rob had of being rescued.

Shortly after Ang Dorje and Lhakpa departed the South Col on their rescue attempt, three other Sherpas, two from Scott's expedition and one from Makalu Gau's team, also left. They were attempting to reach their two leaders, who were stranded some 400 metres above the South Col. When they found the two stranded climbers, Scott was still breathing, but it was clear that there was no chance of saving his life. Makalu Gau, remarkably, after drinking some hot tea and taking in supplementary oxygen, was able to stumble on the end of a short rope down to the South Col.

All of the Sherpas taking part in these two rescue attempts had climbed up the same route the day before. They were making a brave attempt, even though they must have been extremely tired.

It is a fact that Sherpas are generally far stronger than the majority of mountaineers with whom they climb. This is not always the case; there are some outstandingly strong international climbers and, moreover, most of the foreign climbers are technically more skilled than the Sherpas. But when it comes to a rescue attempt, Sherpas are able to make very valuable contributions.

The freshest Sherpas, however, on the South Col that morning were the South African team's Sherpas, who had spent the previous day in their tents while the summit attempts were going on. The Sherpas attached to the Himalayan Guides team were less fresh, having climbed up to the South Col the day before in very difficult conditions. At the least, it would have been expected that the South African Sherpas would have remained to look after their three Western team members. Given their freshness, it would have not been surprising if they had accompanied the two rescue teams, made up of their fellow Sherpas, who were bravely heading upwards – or had even gone up instead of them.

What actually happened was that shortly after the two rescue teams departed, the four South African Sherpas left their three Western team members and departed from the South Col and headed down to Camp 2 and on to Base Camp. Potentially the four freshest and arguably strongest climbers at the South Col had abandoned their fellow mountaineers. Nobody knew what help would be required by those above if, for example, they had managed to bring Scott or Rob down to the South Col. Woodall appeared to subsequently condone the actions of his four Sherpas, but to do otherwise would have shown Woodall in an even worse light. He was their leader and what they did, or did not do, was ultimately his responsibility.

As Neal Beidleman's group descended to Camp 3, they met Pete Athans and Todd Burleson who were on their way up to the South Col to give whatever assistance was needed. Pete and Todd had spent the previous night at Camp 3 while on their own way up for a summit attempt, and they were fortunately in a position to climb relatively quickly to the South Col compared with climbers who were at Camp 2.

It took Neal and his group all day to get down the Lhotse Face. By the time they reached Camp 3, David Breashears was already there having climbed up during the day from Camp 2. Some 200 metres from the bottom of the face they met a group of Sherpas who were on their way to give whatever assistance the Mountain Madness team required. Not long after the two groups met up, and just before it got dark, one of the Sherpas in the rescue team was hit twice by rock fall. The shocked group carried the unconscious climber across the upper section of the Western Cwm to Camp 2 where a medical facility had been established.

The mountain was continuing to grumble.

When Pete and Todd reached the South Col during the morning of 11 May we at last had relatively fresh and very experienced climbers at the col who were able to make sensible decisions. From the time of their arrival, communications between the various camps improved significantly.

Just before Pete and Todd arrived, David Breashears gave permission for those at the South Col to use the IMAX oxygen cylinders which had been previously cached at the team's Camp 4. This was a generous gesture to help to prevent further injury or loss of life, particularly given that David's team were making a film, the subsequent success of which depended on them filming at least some of their team reaching the summit and to do this they needed the oxygen stored at the South Col. When David made his offer to let others use his cached cylinders, there was no way of telling how much oxygen would be used and whether there would be enough left for David's team to succeed with their venture. David also gave permission to let others use his spare batteries for their radios.

The first task undertaken by Pete and Todd was the distribution of batteries and oxygen to those in need, after which they monitored what was happening to the Sherpas above who were still trying to reach Scott, Makalu and Rob.

Just after 3 p.m. the news was received from the south-east ridge that the Sherpas who were bravely trying to reach Rob had been forced to turn back in the face of deteriorating weather. Rob's last chance of being rescued had gone.

At 4.30 p.m. Pete and Todd were standing outside their tent on the South Col when they saw a figure walking towards them. Beck Weathers had risen from his icy grave.

He had been lying in his icy tomb for some seven hours or so when he opened his eyes and became aware of his predicament. He stood and started to move, fortunately in the opposite direction to the Kangshung Face, the sheer drop just beyond his temporary grave. At last he saw what he thought at first were rocks, but as he moved nearer he realised that in front of him were the tents of Camp 4.

How Beck survived will remain a medical mystery. The vast majority of climbers in the same circumstances would have died. It has been speculated that the time Beck spent sitting on the south-east ridge, waiting for Rob to return, had actually saved him. His bodily functions had already slowed down gradually while he was sitting and waiting, and his entombment allowed the functions to slow down even further without completely switching off.

Even though Beck had survived the ordeal of the previous night, he appeared to be in a very grave state. It was decided, this time by several climbers who saw him, that he was unlikely to survive. He was placed in two sleeping bags in an empty tent, with hot water bottles to warm him up further. He was also placed on oxygen.

The decision to put Beck in a tent on his own has always mystified me. I have seen many deaths on and off the mountains. Some people, we knew, were definitely going to die, but we never gave up trying to save them until they had taken their last breath. Beck could have been placed in one of the tents occupied by the other teams at the South Col – having survived in such horrendous circumstances being left to die alone seemed wrong.

That afternoon the Sherpas who had gone to rescue Scott and Makalu arrived back at the South Col with Makalu stumbling behind them. Within a short time, two climbers who could so easily have been dead were still alive. Sadly, the Sherpas also brought the news that Scott was beyond help.

On hearing this news, and with hope that had been fuelled by Beck's survival, Anatoli Boukreev set off up the mountain on a solo attempt to rescue Scott. This was an extremely brave gesture. Darkness was rushing in and the weather was rapidly deteriorating, but this did not stop Anatoli, who reached his friend at 7 p.m. It must have been devastating for Anatoli to discover that Scott was dead.

The weather by this time was worse than it had been the night before. On the South Col tents were being buffeted and flattened. One can only imagine how bad it was for Beck, who was still alone but now much more aware of his predicament. Anatoli descended in the midst of the storm and was lucky to find his way back to the tents.

That day, while these rescue attempts were going on, Guy Cotter had walked from Pumori to Everest Base Camp. Just before 3.30 p.m., not long before Guy and I met to discuss the rescue options, Guy told Rob that the attempt to rescue him that day had failed.

Despite being in the most appalling situation, courageous Rob said that he could survive another night, if help could reach him by 10 a.m. the following day. Given the extreme weather conditions on the upper reaches of the mountain, down at Base Camp we knew that a further rescue mission would be impossible.

At 6.20 p.m. on 11 May, from the Adventure Consultants radio tent from where we were now co-ordinating the rescue, Guy contacted Rob to tell him that his wife Jan was again on the radio from Christchurch. It was the last conversation between a dying man and his wife, and both Rob and Jan probably realised that. Rob closed by imploring Jan not to 'worry too much'.

The majority of what went on during the period of the storm on Everest in May 1996 and the details of the subsequent rescue seem so clear in hindsight. Let me assure all who may one day read this book that, at the time, things on the evening of 11 May were still far from clear. In fact, the expression 'clear as mud' readily springs to mind when I think of what we were facing that night.

At my meeting with Guy shortly before 5 p.m. we spent time discussing how we would organise and co-ordinate a mass casualty evacuation through the Icefall. At that stage we had no real overall idea of who was in what state on the mountain – and the storm was still raging, giving rise to concern that things could only get worse. There were some thirty bridges between the bottom of the Icefall and Camp 2. We had already experienced how long it had taken to bring Ginge Fullen and Kim Sejberg down and it was easy to imagine just how long it would take to bring many casualties down from higher up. Then there was the manpower aspect. It would take far more climbers than were available on the mountain to facilitate a large casualty evacuation. Only some hours before, it had taken eight Sherpas to carry Chen Yu-Nan's body through the Icefall, and live climbers would need more Sherpas to carry them than dead climbers would. We considered our options, which included asking the Nepalese Army to help man the Icefall if the situation got worse.

We also needed a clear understanding of our role. First and foremost we were responsible for supporting the efforts of the rescuers on the mountain. Without any question, we would attempt to provide whatever support was needed by those above. Secondly, we would assess how we could use external support to overcome the problems of getting casualties through the Icefall. This would allow those above to concentrate on getting the injured down to the end of the Western Cwm. Next, we would co-ordinate all communications with the outside world, particularly with the embassies, in respect of the dead and injured. Where necessary we would also deal with the press – little did we know just how much interest would be generated by the unfolding events. Our priority was to get a clear picture of events above us on the mountain.

The first meeting with the Nepalese liaison officers and the support staff of each expedition was going to be the most important. We had to make sure that everyone at Base Camp had a clear understanding of what was going on and what was required from them.

I also had the problem of imposing some direction on those at the meeting; I hardly knew many of those present. For me, there was an urgent need to get things quickly organised to support those above. I didn't have time for niceties; someone had to take an immediate grip of the situation. This was, in fact, not a problem. There was an evident desire among those at Base Camp for someone to direct them and there was not a single murmur of dissent as I opened that first formal meeting.

At the meeting there were representatives of all the teams on Everest and all the liaison officers (LOs). I made a particular effort to acknowledge the senior liaison officer. The goodwill of the local liaison officers would have helped, but trying to make them feel that they were an essential part of the rescue team turned out to be a waste of time. From that meeting onwards, all the LOs seemed to do, whenever I saw them, was moan.

I told all the team representatives that I wanted a list of all their climbers who were on the mountain and I wanted to know what their status was – where they were, and if they were dead, injured (and if so how badly were they injured), or okay. I wanted this information within one hour.

I also strongly suggested that we impose a communications embargo with the outside world. We had already started to inform the various embassies in Kathmandu when we had definite information to be passed on to the relatives of the dead. But until we had confirmation that the relatives had been informed, or until the picture became clearer, I did not want the breaking news to worry the thousands of friends and relatives of the climbers on Everest that year. There was another reason for this – I didn't want our limited communications to become jammed by thousands of calls coming into Base Camp from the outside world.

We needed the information about the status of the climbers as quickly as possible and I didn't want to detain those who were at the meeting. Before they departed, I asked the senior LO if he could obtain a weather forecast from Nepalese sources which would give us a clearer picture of how things were likely to develop during the next day or so. The response that followed from the senior LO had to be cut short. Instead of immediately getting on with obtaining the weather forecast, he remained in the tent and launched into a speech about the inaccuracy of the weather reports which had been obtained by the Danish members of Mal's team.

These daily reports arrived via the satellite phone from the British Meteorological Office in Bracknell, in the UK. Mal had helped to organise this and the Danes had paid to receive the information while they were on the mountain. The information was then sold on to other teams to cover the Danes' initial investment. The information was also widely leaked and virtually all the teams on Everest knew what the forecasts said, whether or not they had paid for them.

These forecasts were for five-day periods and were wildly inaccurate. They gave an indication of the temperature and the speed and direction of the wind that we could expect at 7,000 metres and on the summit, but not what we would experience lower on the mountain.

It became a joke among the climbers that the weather prediction had been sent to the wrong Danish mountaineering team and was meant for another mountain, because rarely did the actual weather resemble that which had been forecast. But in the absence of forecasts from closer to Everest, this was the best that could be done.

This forecast was simply intended to give information for Everest. It did not warn us of any storms outside of the Everest region which might impact on us – a significant omission, given what had happened on 10 May. And this was the point of the senior LO's speech – he wanted to blame the whole affair on Western technology.

He may have had a point, but it was not the time or the place to debate the issue. What I needed was action – to provide a forecast for the next few days from whatever source the LO could contact. I was wasting my breath and all the LOs seemed to do was to descend into a childlike huff, which they significantly failed to come out of over the next few days. It seemed to particularly rile them that I could understand their language and they were unable to discuss points during the meetings privately between themselves before their chosen spokesman launched into the series of moans that became a regular feature of our meetings.

We agreed to have our next formal meeting at 8 a.m. on 12 May and the team representatives hurried to get the information we required in the meantime.

I set about drawing up the chart on which the status of all climbers on the mountain would be recorded. Göran Kropp, who was still recovering at Base Camp, suggested that we should draw a plan of Everest and write the names of climbers where they were located on the mountain. This idea had merit, but it was felt to be too complicated. At some locations, mainly by this time at Camp 2, there were dozens of climbers and the map of the mountain would need to be very large if we were going to fit them all in. There was also the problem of recording their status, which we so desperately needed, in order to have a clear idea of the size of the problem facing us. We therefore agreed to only plot the climbers above Camp 2 for the time being.

That is, in essence, how we worked throughout the next three days, particularly Guy and me. We discussed ideas and options, until we came up with what we thought was the best plan. The overriding consideration was simply that anything was worth trying if it was going to make things easier for the rescuers on the mountain.

Within the hour, all the team representatives had returned to give their report. The information was transferred to the chart and at last we had the first overall picture of the status of everyone on the mountain above Camp 2.

The information in front of us gave us an idea of what we faced. We now knew that Doug Hansen, Yasuko Namba and Scott Fischer were, in all probability, dead. Rob Hall was unlikely to survive much longer; in view of the conditions on the mountain it was amazing that he had survived this long. Andy Harris was missing, presumed dead, having fallen, we assumed, down the south-west face of Everest. There were several reports of frostbite, but in all cases the person concerned could walk; this was the same for those with varying degrees of snow blindness. The only two casualties who would require a major effort to get them off the mountain appeared to be Beck Weathers and Makalu Gau, both of whom were now in tents at the South Col.

It was a long night. Most of us had slept little during the previous forty-eight hours, but strangely we were not aware of being tired. We sat, chatted and monitored the radio, but there was little we could do except wait to see what the morning would bring.

10

THE DESIRE TO LIVE

Those who spent the night of 11–12 May on the South Col included Pete, Todd and Anatoli, the survivors of the Adventure Consultants team, the South Africans and the clients from the Himalayan Guides expedition. By the time dawn broke on the morning of 12 May, for many at the South Col it was the third night that they had spent there or on the ridge above. For much of this time they had not slept much; they were in a state of extreme exhaustion and it was vital that they descend without delay.

As soon as it got light, the climbers started to prepare to descend. At 8.30 a.m. the remnants of the Adventure Consultants team started down. This did not look like the same team which had, only a relatively short time before, made its way up the mountain from Base Camp, full of confidence and ambition.

Between before midnight and 8.30 a.m. no climber at the South Col had gone to see whether or not Beck was still alive – it was probable that Beck had died, but no one knew for sure. But Beck had survived and, finding that he was still alive, his teammate Jon Krakauer rushed over to Pete and Todd, who started to give Beck the help he so desperately needed.

Earlier that morning the Taiwanese Sherpas had started to descend with Makalu Gau. It was going to be a cold and painful descent for Makalu. He was very badly frostbitten and without the aid of his loyal Sherpas he would not have made it back to Camp 2 that day.

Following in the tracks of the remaining members of Rob Hall's team came the South Africans, followed later by the Himalayan Guides team, who had at last decided to give up their summit attempt.

On the South Col, Pete and Todd continued to look after Beck. The day had dawned clear, but the winds were horrendous. Only when climbers reached the Lhotse Face would they get any relief from the force of the storm.

Amazingly, Beck was able to eat and drink and, after taking some drugs, the speed of his recovery amazed both Pete and Todd. By mid-morning he was dressed and ready to go and, most surprisingly, he could walk.

Despite Beck's appalling injuries, his good humour and positive attitude were an inspiration to all who met him during his evacuation from the mountain. As a doctor, Beck could appreciate the extent of his problems – he would later have his lower right arm amputated, and he would lose the fingers and thumb on his left hand and most of his nose.

Pete and Todd escorted Beck through the wind and down towards the Lhotse Face.

At the Yellow Band they were met by the Austrian climber Robert Schauer and the American Ed Viesturs, both members of the IMAX team who were playing such a vital role in the rescue on the mountain.

Further down at Camp 3, two other members of the IMAX team, the Spanish climber Araceli Segarra and the American team leader David Breashears, were waiting to give whatever further assistance was required. Also there was the Finnish climber, Veikka Gustafsson, and the American guide Jim Williams, who was climbing with Todd.

At Camp 2, the Adventure Consultants dining tent had been converted into a first aid medical centre. It was manned by the Danish doctor Henrik Jessen Hansen, one of the Danish climbers on our International Team, and by Todd Burleson's American team doctor, Ken Kamler.

At about 1 p.m., the South African team, the members of the Himalayan Guides team who had been on the South Col, and the remnants of the Adventure Consultants team staggered slowly into Camp 2.

Now the only groups above Camp 2 were the rescue parties bringing down Makalu and Beck.

At 3 p.m. the first of these two groups, the one escorting Makalu Gau, arrived at the temporary medical centre. The doctors were amazed at the extent of Makalu's frostbite. Within ninety minutes he would be joined by Beck Weathers.

The speed at which Beck was able to walk down to Camp 2 from the bottom of the Lhotse Face surprised everyone that day. It was difficult to believe that just over twenty-four hours earlier he had been lying alone in a cold, icy grave, having been given up for dead. He still had to face a night on his own in a tent that was being assaulted by the full force of a storm. It wasn't until some seven hours or so before he arrived at Camp 2 that Beck at last proved to his fellow climbers that he really was going to survive.

That night the two doctors at Camp 2 started the slow process of thawing out Makalu and Beck's frozen limbs.

It had been forty-eight hours from the time those at Camp 2 had first realised that things on the mountain were going horribly wrong until the arrival of Beck and Makalu. During those forty-eight hours none of the climbers at Camp 2 had slept much and they were all on the verge of mental exhaustion. It was amazing what a revitalising effect the arrival of these two climbers had at Camp 2. There was still some way to go, and things could still go wrong, but it was a significantly better atmosphere than it had been two days before when a sense of gloom prevailed.

11

THE HEIGHT OF PETTINESS

The news that Beck was alive was quickly sent to the American embassy in Kathmandu, where it was relayed to his family in the States – what a harrowing few hours they must have had since they were informed that he was thought to be dead.

From our perspective at Base Camp the picture on the mountain was at last becoming clear and we could concentrate on making plans to get Beck and Makalu down through the Icefall to Base Camp.

It was Guy Cotter who suggested using a helicopter to bring them down from Camp 1. From my time as a helicopter pilot in the British Army, I thought that it would be very difficult for a helicopter to land and take off at the height of Camp 1 on the edge of the Western Cwm.

I have been asked many times since 1996 why a helicopter didn't rescue Rob Hall at over 8,000 metres. Quite simply, and without going into complex technical explanations, the air is too thin. Most military helicopters at the time had height limits somewhere around 5,000 metres. It was bad enough that Camp 1 was over 6,000 metres and the helicopter wasn't just going to have to fly at that height, it was also going to land and take off – twice.

There were also the problems of flying in mountainous terrain, where strange and powerful wind conditions can cause additional problems.

Despite the limitations, a helicopter had tried to land in the Western Cwm in 1973 when an Italian Army expedition climbed the mountain. After the helicopter had crashed making an attempt to land, the team were forced to porter their stores up through the Icefall. It was some small coincidence that I had climbed with some of the Italians from that expedition in the early 1970s, but it never occurred to me in those distant days that twenty-two years later the fact that their helicopter had crashed would once again be useful information.

The idea of using a helicopter was discussed with Kathmandu and an experienced Nepalese Army pilot, Lieutenant Colonel Madan Khatri Chhetri, volunteered to have a go. The attempt was scheduled for the morning of 13 May.

At my initial meeting on 11 May I had tried to impose a communications ban with the outside world, but it was clear by the next day that a flood of information was leaving Base Camp. It was pointless investigating who the culprit was; I suspect there was more than one. Most teams had satellite telephones at Base Camp through which, in most cases, emails or faxes could be sent. Several teams had direct links to the media and it would have been a great temptation to relay information to the outside world.

Rather than let what was apparently misleading news trickle out and, given that we had a fair idea now who was dead, we decided to issue an accurate press release. There was also a need to reassure the friends and relatives of survivors on the mountain that their loved ones were okay.

This was, however, not our only communications problem. The head LO came to see me to complain that while the outside world was starting to hear about events on Everest, the ministry in Kathmandu were still largely in the dark. I found some sympathy with this problem. As the news started to leak, the world's press were starting to seek information from the government in Kathmandu. Unfortunately the LOs had no direct link with their headquarters and by the morning of 12 May they had only been able to pass on limited information. Embarrassment was being caused when it became apparent that the members of the world's press corps who were phoning in knew more about events than the government officials responsible for mountaineering in Nepal.

I organised for the LOs to have greater access to a satellite phone to keep their ministry updated. This was, however, a further deterioration in the relationship between the rescue co-ordinators and the LOs because they resented that we had control of equipment and they had to always seek our help to contact their ministry.

Throughout the day, as we heard that Beck and Makalu were being brought down to Camp 2, the mood at Base Camp lightened. It was too early for the outpouring of grief that was to come two days later. For a short time the dead were forgotten and we focused on the miracle that two climbers had survived.

We still had to get them down to Base Camp and out to Kathmandu, but this would be a lot simpler than getting them down from Camp 4 to Camp 1.

12

HELICOPTER TO THE RESCUE

About 7 a.m. on the morning of 13 May 1996 we heard the distant sound of an approaching helicopter. These machines had constantly flown into Base Camp during the previous weeks and it became a game to see who could spot the aircraft first. The sound of its engines always reached us long before we got our first glimpse.

As the helicopter circled Base Camp, I still had my doubts about its ability to lift the casualties to the valley from the top of the Icefall. After the helicopter landed on the prepared area at the bottom of the camp, and under the instruction of the pilot Colonel Madan, we helped to lift all removable items from the interior of the Squirrel aircraft to reduce the weight to an absolute minimum.

Above us, at first light, Beck and Makalu had been helped down the Western Cwm. Makalu, who was unable to walk, was put on a plastic stretcher and dragged down the cwm. Getting him across the bridges was difficult, but the Sherpas who brought him down worked with the satisfaction that this was a life plucked from death. Those in front crossed and held the ropes taught as the stretcher was guided over the ladders that spanned the gaps.

Beck was able to stumble down despite his horrific injuries and he was helped by some of those who had played such an important role in the overall rescue during the last two days.

At the bottom of the Western Cwm, close to Camp 1, Kool-Aid was used to mark the point where the helicopter was to land to pick up Beck and Makalu.

From below we saw the Squirrel disappear into the cwm, but then it almost immediately reappeared – Colonel Madan was clearly taking no chances. He spent several minutes judging the wind direction and reconnoitring the proposed landing site. Landing would not be too difficult – my helicopter flying instructor had always told me that landings were always, in effect, controlled crashes – but taking off would be much more difficult at that height with the extra weight.

At last Colonel Madan committed himself to the landing and he made his approach to the selected landing site. Makalu was placed first in the helicopter and Colonel Madan lifted slightly to make full use of the ground cushion which was being created by the air being sucked down through the rotor blades on to the snow. He crept forward and gradually increased speed so that the airflow over the blades would create lift. As he got to the lip of the cwm he was able to safely fly downwards to create extra speed and, in doing so, extra lift. It was a remarkable feat of flying at the edge of the capability of the helicopter he was piloting.

With some relief we watched the Squirrel spiralling down to us and as it landed we rushed forward to help unload Makalu. At the same time the watching LOs who had waited at the helicopter landing point also rushed forward, but not to help Makalu. Instead they lined up in front of the helicopter while a co-opted Sherpa took their photograph. This summarised more clearly than anything the role the group of Nepalese liaison officers played during the rescue.

Makalu was wrapped up and was breathing oxygen and it was impossible to tell just how bad he was. The joy of his fellow team members at Base Camp was evident and Makalu's fellow Taiwanese Base Camp manager, who had lost all his fingers during their training climb on McKinley, grasped my hand between his two stumps and pumped my hand vigorously.

While Makalu sat on the side of the landing site the helicopter returned to pick up Beck. This time Colonel Madan was less cautious with his approach and within minutes he had landed back at Base Camp with Beck. We loaded Makalu into the back of the helicopter and replaced the various items we had removed in order to lighten the aircraft not long before. Shortly afterwards, the helicopter lifted skywards, and Makalu and Beck were on their way to Kathmandu.

Despite some teams not taking part in the rescue and the completely unhelpful part played by the Nepalese liaison officers, for those who did selflessly play their part, the rescue of Beck and Makalu meant a great deal. Now the grieving for lost friends could start.

My last task at Base Camp when all the teams had returned was to chair a meeting where we discussed how the other teams could replace the oxygen which the IMAX team had donated to the rescue. And then it was time to leave – my chest condition was now so bad there was no chance of me going high again. I felt nothing, neither sadness, nor disappointment or any other conceivable emotion. I just wanted to return to my home, where I would be able to make some sense of what had happened.

Within a period of a little over six years after the tragedy, a further seven climbers who were on the south side of Everest that year were to die. The first of these deaths happened on 25 May 1996.

After the departure of most of the teams, the South Africans made a summit attempt in late May, which yet again caused controversy. In O'Dowd's words she, Woodall and Herrod left Camp 4 at around midnight on the night of 24–25 May, together with three Sherpas. After an uneventful climb, Woodall and O'Dowd both reached the summit – according to their own reports at 10 a.m., accompanied by one of their three Sherpas. O'Dowd later said that on the descent they passed the other two Sherpas just before the South Summit, and Bruce Herrod just after they came over the top of the South Summit. They had a talk with Herrod, before he continued upwards. It should take about two hours for a healthy and fit climber to reach the top from the South Summit, but, for reasons which will never be known, Bruce didn't get there until 5 p.m. We will never know what happened next, but Bruce's body was found a year later hanging on the ropes at the Hillary Step.

Woodall received some criticism for not trying hard enough to turn Herrod around, but given how much Bruce wanted to reach the top, it would have been difficult to stop him. What I think is more questionable is how Woodall organised his Sherpas. There were three climbers and three Sherpas, and it would have been appropriate and sensible with the availability of such a perfect ratio of Sherpas to climbers to allocate one Sherpa to support each of the climbers. This ratio of one Sherpa to one climber was far better than will be found in most teams on Everest, and given the lack of experience amongst the South African team and what had happened some two weeks earlier during the storm, it would have been such a simple thing to have got right. Instead, the order in which they went to the summit, with Woodall out in front with a Sherpa, followed some way behind by O'Dowd on her own, with two Sherpas more than an hour behind her, followed some way behind by Herrod, demonstrated inexperience and arguably a lack of respect for what they were facing. It is not clear what happened when the second and third Sherpas passed Herrod on their way back from the mountain, which must have been very late in the climbing day, but we do know that Bruce reached the summit at 5 p.m. with no chance of getting far down the mountain before day turned to night.

In September 1996, during the post-monsoon climbing season on Everest, Lopsang Jangbu Sherpa become the second of the climbers who had survived the Everest storm to subsequently die. Whilst working for a Japanese expedition, he was swept to his death in an avalanche high on the Lhotse Face, along with two other mountaineers.

One of the questions I was asked on my return from the mountain, by several ill-informed members of the media, was 'should climbing on Everest be more controlled?' Of course, they were referring to the reports that some of the climbers lacked the necessary experience and should, therefore, have not been allowed to climb the mountain. But perhaps the tragedy was a result of climbing having already become too controlled by commercial interests. Climbers had, in effect, been herded up the mountain instead of being able to break into small groups of climbers who could climb at a similar speed. The idea that climbers, particularly in large groups, can be guided to the top of the world's highest mountain, took a knock that day.

The very nature of the tragedy, with all those involved spread over the mountain, has led to a number of conflicting views – and I acknowledge that mine is just one of them, developed from my own experiences recorded in my diary at the time and what others told me of their experiences. That there were different interpretations of events should not be surprising, these were men and women fighting for their lives in extreme circumstances and others were viewing what was happening from different parts of an 8,848-metre-high mountain. If they had all viewed the same events, at the same time, from the same place on the mountain, as they moved together in one group up and down the route, maybe a more accurate picture of events that day could have been put together. But they didn't, and the inevitable result was the creation of different opinions.

There were two elements which I believe led to the tragedy that day. One was the weather, the other was a decision-making process which, once started, could not be halted, because humans often still don't know when to turn back in order to live another day – a similar trait which led to deaths in the Fastnet storm some seventeen years before.

Audrey Salkeld, later in an article titled 'Emergency on Everest' in the *Alpine Journal,* was to generously say, 'The only good thing to come out of the whole tragic business is the wonderful co-operation that so quickly built up among the rescuers, and the superb co-ordination notably by Helen Wilton, Guy Cotter and Mike Trueman at Base and the mountaineers on the mountain.'

There is no doubt that there were many brave acts high on the mountain, but we were, in my view, simply there to support those above.

On my return from Everest I grieved and then got on with my life and made plans for further expeditions.

13

AN ADVENTUROUS SABBATICAL

In 1989 I had put in an application to leave the army, but a colleague in the Ministry of Defence passed me the word that redundancy would soon be offered to officers in the British Forces. At the same time I was offered a position in the team being sent to Namibia to train their new army in preparation for the country's independence. This job would last for a year and I knew that command of the Army Mountain Training Centre (AMTC) in Germany would become available at about that time. I agreed to go to Namibia on condition that I would then get command of AMTC – this was readily agreed to. I also knew that redundancy would be available in 1992 when my time at AMTC was due to come to an end, and for the first time in my army career I had a good idea what I would be doing for the next three years.

My year in Namibia was wonderful. Whilst I was based in the capital Windhoek, my particular job meant that I spent a great deal of time roaming throughout this amazing land. The flight out from London was full of junior diplomats who were going out to set up their new embassies prior to independence. It was very much a party atmosphere on the plane as we all walked around the cabin with drinks, chatting excitedly about being there as the world's newest independent country was born. I started talking to two gentlemen, one of whom asked me what I was going to be doing in Namibia, and I explained that I was part of the British Army Training Team, to which he replied that he had heard about us. I then asked him what he was going to be doing to which he replied, 'I am the new prime minister.' In the weeks ahead I would learn to recognise Hage Geingob who was destined to be Namibia's prime minister from 1990 to 2002. Needless to say, after our meeting on the aircraft, I didn't meet him again.

We did, however, get to attend the independence ceremony. It was surreal sitting there in front of Archbishop Desmond Tutu with Yasser Arafat and Colonel Gaddafi only a few feet away. But the star of the show was Nelson Mandela, who had only been released from prison a month before. The ceremony ended in true African style when South African president de Klerk abruptly ended his speech because, in his words, it was past midnight and Namibia had been independent for five minutes, but the South African flag was still flying instead of the new flag of the new nation.

For anyone who likes a wild landscape Namibia has it all and I could not have been happier. Even during my weekends off I would drive into the desert, or through the numerous game reserves, marvelling at what this country had to offer. One of my favourite spots was Sossusvlei on the edge of the Namib Desert with its towering sand dunes reaching over 300 metres in height. I would regularly drive there after work on a Friday night to camp on the edge of the desert before reaching the dunes in time for sunrise.

Namibia had been a German colony until the First World War and even in the late twentieth century there were lots of reminders of this legacy. In particular, the very orderly way of life compared with other African countries, including several first class restaurants, which offered a very pleasant evening out when I wasn't travelling. One of the odd results of sanctions against South Africa was that the country could not export much of its wine and the best of this wine was available at restaurants in Windhoek at a fraction of the price it would reach in later years.

Namibia was also a huge and sparsely populated country, twice the size of France and, with a population of only a little over one million in 1990, most of the country was isolated and uninhabited. There were stories that some Nazis had escaped to Namibia (or South-West Africa as it was at the time) at the end of the Second World War and bizarrely in the coastal town of Swakopmund members of the white population still celebrated Hitler's birthday during my time in the country.

I could have happily stayed in the country for a lot longer than a year, but life moves on, and from the wilds of Africa I moved to command the AMTC which was based in the Harz mountains in the north of Germany. At the end of the Second World War the Americans occupied the south of Germany with its excellent skiing and mountaineering and the British got the industrial north of the country with its limited scope for adventure. We did get some regular snowfall in the Harz which enabled the centre to offer cross-country skiing and, less frequently, downhill skiing courses in winter, as well as rock-climbing and canoeing courses all year round. The remainder of the courses were held in Bavaria, Austria and France, and I spent a great deal of time travelling down to the Alps and back.

Following on from the super time I had in Namibia, my two years in command of AMTC, where I spent the majority of my time skiing and mountaineering, were a perfect end to my twenty-four years in the army. And, in addition, the payment I received when I was made redundant was significantly more than I would have got had my resignation been accepted two years previously.

After leaving the army in 1992 I initially went to work in Yugoslavia for the British Foreign Office as part of the European Community Monitor Mission, whose mandate was to monitor borders, inter-ethnic relations, refugee traffic and political and security developments. We operated throughout the war-torn former states that had previously made up Yugoslavia and, in order to identify us as being neutral, we wore an all-white uniform, which made us look like cricket players in the middle of a war zone.

It was a fascinating, but also on occasions a sad job. One of my first tasks was to find out what happened to hundreds of citizens of Vukovar who had disappeared at the end of an eighty-seven-day siege the previous year. It seems unbelievable that almost 300 people could disappear in Europe at the end of the twentieth century, but that is what happened. It would be over ten years before members of the Yugoslav People's Army and

Serb paramilitaries responsible for what became known as the Vukovar massacre were brought to trial.

The pace of work as a monitor could on occasions be slow, but it was never boring. On one occasion I went, accompanied by a Russian army colonel who was working with the UN, to witness a prisoner exchange between the Croatian and Serbian forces. As we crossed 'no man's land', we were suddenly surrounded by Serbian special forces who had been hiding in the undergrowth. I was held at gunpoint with an AK47 pointing at my head. The EU were seen to be siding with Croatia and I was being berated by a very angry and menacing Serb special forces commander. Fortunately, after a tense couple of minutes, the Russian colonel came to my rescue, but I remain convinced that if he hadn't been there I would in all likelihood have been shot, which would have made a real mess of my white uniform.

It wasn't all gloom. Towards the end of my one year in the role, we thought that Croatia might cross Hungarian territory to attack Serbia and I was sent to the very pleasant Hungarian border town of Szeged to monitor the situation. For some two months I toured southern Hungary as well as exploring Budapest – if I had to work in a war zone, this was a very pleasant way to do it.

After finishing with the monitor mission I worked as logistics co-ordinator for the European Humanitarian Office, based in Belgrade, during which time I was responsible for thousands of displaced persons through-out Serbia.

Even during the war I found time to visit the mountains, but walks were more often limited by minefields than they were by bad weather.

14

CHOMOLUNGMA CONTINUES TO RUMBLE

I returned to Hong Kong after Everest 1996, combining my job in corporate affairs in the container terminal with my twice-yearly expeditions to the Himalaya. It was a strange but exciting time to live in the territory; the military connection which I had been part of – or associated with – for twenty years was coming to an end and there was a mixture of excitement caused by the change from British to Chinese rule, as well as concern, primarily amongst the Chinese part of the population, many of whom were emigrating to Canada and Australia, because they thought that after the handover they would be ruled by a repressive regime.

Most visitors only see the frenetically busy city areas of Hong Kong, which are amongst the most densely populated parts of the world. However, beyond the concrete jungles which lie along the harbour side of Hong Kong Island and across the harbour on the Kowloon Peninsula is a range of hills, which although not dramatically high, offer stunning walks. I was lucky enough to live close to the hills, through which I would go for long daily runs. Most weekends found me trekking through the hills, often visiting small Chinese seafood restaurants in remote villages which could only be reached by foot or by boat. It was a wonderful way to spend down-time while maintaining fitness, despite everything that had happened the previous year.

In 1997 I returned to Everest. The tragic events of the year before seemed a lifetime ago – life goes on – but how quickly the memory of climbers, who had died on the same mountain I was climbing, fades.

My son Dan flew with me to Kathmandu. He had been unable to join his brother Tom and sister Nicole when they trekked with me into Base

Camp in 1996 because of his final school exams. The plan was for Dan to join me at Base Camp after trekking around Annapurna.

The 1997 season was always going to be pot luck for me because I had commitments which meant I could only remain at Base Camp until 20 May. If I hadn't reached the top by then, my 1997 Everest attempt would be over.

On arriving in Kathmandu I was interested to find that I was being considered for the position of managing director of arguably the most established mountaineering agency in Kathmandu. This was something I had not previously considered and it was a pleasant boost to my ego, but running a busy agency would have meant fewer opportunities to take part in expeditions, given that I would be busy organising them for others. Also, as much as I liked Kathmandu, every time I arrived in Nepal I spent as little time in the city as I could, wanting to get into the mountains as quickly as possible. The thought of spending most of my time in Kathmandu was not overly attractive and I politely declined the job offer.

I was climbing again with Mal Duff and the two of us met up in Namche Bazaar en route to Everest. Mal was in good form but I recorded in my diary that he seemed to have something on his mind, which was not surprising, given everything that goes into running an expedition.

I felt fitter in 1997 than I had the year before, but I purposely took my time walking up to Base Camp and spent two days in the Khumjung valley, which is reached after a steep half day's walk from Namche Bazaar. Often missed by trekkers who take the main path to the east, the Khumjung valley is full of Sherpa houses, each with its own area for cultivation – a sight which has probably changed little over the centuries. What has changed is the Khumjung Secondary School, which has benefitted Sherpa children since it was founded by Edmund Hillary in 1961, and further across the valley is the Khunde Hospital, which was built by Hillary and completed in 1966, bringing much needed medical support within reach of this Sherpa community. The valley's monastery also has a skull purported to be from a yeti. It is arguably more likely to have been the skull of a large monkey, but why let the truth get in the way when donations made by visitors to see this artefact more than pay for the upkeep of the monastery?

For visitors who really want to step back in time there is the Sherpa Heritage House, the former home of my good friend and mountaineering legend Pertemba Sherpa. In 1975, Pertemba was the lead Sherpa on Chris Bonington's south-west face expedition, on which British climbers finally reached the summit of Everest. It was on 24 September 1975 that Doug Scott and Dougal Haston reached the summit, followed two days later by Peter Boardman, Pertemba and Mick Burke (Burke disappeared in worsening weather, presumably later on the descent). Pertemba went on to climb Everest on two further occasions, including in 1985 when he reached the summit with Chris Bonington, and he was also chosen to trek with Prince Charles on the route north of Pokhara which was subsequently named the Royal Trek.

Not everyone visits the Khumjung to experience its cultural heritage and for many climbers it is the German bakery which is the main attraction. At sea level I personally avoid pastries, but at almost 4,000 metres, fresh bread and wonderful pizzas become very tasty, particularly when the diet for the next six weeks is going to consist of bland mountaineering rations.

As I walked up to the monastery at Tengboche I met an old Japanese climbing friend who I had last climbed with in Japan some fifteen years before. He had lost all of his toes as a result of frostbite on a winter ascent of the Matterhorn, and I remember when we had climbed together in the Japanese Alps in 1982 that he claimed the lack of toes in his boots made it easier to make a firmer contact on rock ledges – something I preferred to take his word for.

Mal was leading two teams that year, one climbing Everest by the south-east ridge, and a second, larger team, climbing Lhotse – a climb which shares the route up Everest until a point midway between Camp 3 and the Geneva Spur, from where those climbing Lhotse climb directly upwards to their summit. Our Everest team that year, besides Mal and me, included three Mexicans and Brigitte Muir, who was aiming to be the first Australian woman to reach the highest point on earth.

It was great to be back and to greet many old friends at Base Camp who had been there in 1996. On 16 April I started up through the Icefall for the first time that year. Either I was fitter or the Icefall was more welcoming, but I found it a lot easier than I had the year before, although I did have a moment of frightening excitement when a ledge I was standing on collapsed. Fortunately I was jumaring up a fixed rope at the time and I just had to haul my way up the rope to safety.

The theory of acclimatisation on Everest is to climb high and then descend back to a lower camp to sleep and to then gradually move up to higher camps. Everest has been climbed in April, but over the years, particularly as commercial expeditions gained momentum in the 1990s, the majority of ascents have occurred from the second week of May onwards. The limiting factors are that the monsoon can start to hit the mountain during this period if it arrives early, and the permit to climb Everest in the spring runs out on 1 June.

After spending a night at Camp 1, which was in a similar location to the previous year, I walked up to Camp 2 and back the next day, and then spent a very stormy night back at Camp 1. It felt like a very good introduction to that year's expedition. The following day it took me only two hours to get back down to Base Camp, passing Mal in the Icefall, as well as Gary Guller, an American climber on the Lhotse team who had had an arm amputated following a climbing accident some years before. I always found Gary to be very cheerful and ever confident, despite how difficult he must have found it to climb through the labyrinth of the Icefall with only one arm, and I wished him well as I romped downhill.

Long gone are the days when the only way to communicate from Everest, or from any other mountain in Nepal, was to use a Sherpa runner. Depending on where in Nepal you were, the Sherpa would run (actually walk fast rather than run, but the Sherpas walk at a pace through the hills at which most mortals would have to run to keep up with them) back to Kathmandu where the message would be phoned, or in later times faxed, through to the overseas recipient. Once a reply was received the Sherpa would then run back to Base Camp and, depending on where in Nepal you were located, it took some ten days or so from the initial writing of the message until the reply was received. In 1992, I dealt with most of the paperwork to buy my house in France by this method. Modern communications have developed swiftly since the early 1990s and the use of satellites has meant that phones and internet connections are now fundamental pieces of expedition equipment.

It was a balance to decide when to phone or send an email, but often the news of an accident on Everest, which we knew the outside world would quickly hear about, was a catalyst to send a quick message of some sort back to family or friends to make sure they knew I was still alive.

My plan was to climb back up on 21 April and to then spend six days on the mountain, mostly at Camp 2 with an excursion up the Lhotse Face to Camp 3. I couldn't get over how fit I felt and I climbed from Base Camp to Camp 1 in three hours, which was good for that stage of the acclimatisation process, particularly as I had another minor epic en route. While I was crossing a crevasse on a bridge made up of three ladders tied together, one of my crampons became jammed between two of the ladders where they were tied together by rope, and I became stuck halfway across, looking down below my feet through the rungs of the ladder into a dark abyss. In front of some American climbers who were waiting at the side of the crevasse to cross, I tried to look as cool as possible as I stooped down and unclipped from the offending crampon. I then bent down again to pick up the crampon and continued the crossing. Whilst feeling somewhat unnerved inside, my performance gave rise to one of the watching Americans declaring, 'Gee, that was impressive.' It may well have been, but it was something I had no wish to repeat.

But Everest can be fickle. On 22 April I moved from Camp 1 up to Camp 2 with a very heavy load, and despite previously feeling strong and fit, I found the last 200 metres up to the camp exhausting. The uninitiated often talk about mountaineers 'conquering mountains', which, in my view, is rubbish. Mountains have to be respected and can't be conquered. It is more accurate to say that climbers sneak up when the mountain has its back turned – we had seen the year before what can happen when the mountain is not looking the other way.

On 23 April I tried to radio Base Camp on schedule at 8 a.m. and at 9 a.m., but there was no reply, which was very unusual. At 10 a.m. I at last got through and I heard the news that Mal had been found dead in his tent in Base Camp that morning. I was in shock; I had chatted to Mal when we passed each other as I was climbing up through the Icefall, and I was waiting for him to join me at Camp 2, having just cleared a space in the tent for him. He had seemed tired during the early part of the expedition, but that is not unusual on Everest, and it certainly hadn't given rise to any concerns. As far as I was aware he was fit and healthy. When Mick Burns radioed from Base Camp to give me the news, he obviously heard the shock and disbelief in my voice because he got another member of the team to speak to me to confirm that it was true – Mal was dead.

I walked over and talked to David Breashears and Pete Athans, also back on the mountain that year, both of whom knew Mal well and who were very understanding when I told them the news. I continued to feel numb throughout the remainder of the day – but there was nothing I could do. The expedition would continue and part of my task while at Camp 2 was to support two of our team who were at Camp 3 and this is what I now focused on doing.

It transpired that down at Base Camp that morning the cook boy had gone to give Mal his early morning cup of tea but when he found he couldn't wake Mal, he had called Mick Burns, our Base Camp manager, who found Mal dead in his sleeping bag. Doctors who were at Base Camp were then called to confirm the death. Sadly rumours quickly spread that Mal had died after choking on his vomit after drinking alcohol and, although I wasn't there at the time, those who found Mal later confirmed that this was nonsense. It was later suggested that he had banged his head in Kathmandu before coming to the mountain and in all likelihood this, and the subsequent effort of climbing at altitude, had caused a brain haemorrhage.

The time in Kathmandu at the start of any expedition gave the opportunity for a last drinking session before the period of abstinence on expedition. At the end of the evening it was not unusual to hire bicycle rickshaws and to get the Nepalese driver to sit in the back while inebriated expedition members sat on the driver's saddle and raced each other through the streets of Kathmandu, which fortunately were often relatively traffic-free at that time of night. Apparently prior to travelling to Base Camp, and whilst taking part in a bicycle rickshaw race, Mal had crashed his cycle and banged his head in the process.

Mal ran an expedition company because it enabled him to climb and to make a living out of mountaineering at the same time. More so than many other climbers that I have known, Mal simply loved to climb and he certainly didn't have the ambition to make large sums of money, which was starting to be reflected by the sums being charged by other companies. To me he was a Scottish climber of the same ilk as Tom Patey, Robin Smith and Dougal Haston, and British climbing had lost one of its great characters. Mal was intelligent, erudite and a great companion to be with in the mountains, and I was one of many who would miss him.

Mal's body was due to be flown out to Kathmandu the following day. The Sherpas put a flask of tea next to the body and a lamp on in the tent, to burn through the night. They then sewed up the flap of the tent, to be opened just before Mal was carried to the helicopter early the following morning.

The following day, British Mountaineer Alan Hinkes, who was climbing Lhotse as part of his quest to become Britain's first mountaineer to summit all fourteen 8,000 metre peaks, joined me in the tent at Camp 2. Al was a fresh air freak, which I was not, and that night he opened his end of the tent, which then felt to me like we were sleeping in a high-altitude wind tunnel. Eventually I got to sleep only to be wakened by Al who told me that I was snoring, to which I abruptly replied, 'It was because I was asleep!'

On 25 April I returned to Base Camp to formally take over leadership of the expedition from Mal. It was not something I wanted to do, but Mal was a friend and someone had to take responsibility for the expedition. I also felt strongly that it was important to finish what Mal had started. We had a very strong team of Sherpas to support the expedition, most of whom I had worked with the year before, and I felt that it would not be too onerous a task to fulfil, and I didn't feel, at that stage, that it would have any impact on my own climb to the summit. I also heard from Liz, Mal's wife, who had arrived in Nepal to escort his body back to Scotland.

Liz now ran Mal's climbing company and she also asked me to take on the leadership role. Liz had herself climbed high on the Tibetan side of Everest, as well as becoming the first British woman to summit Pumori, a climb she had made with Mal in 1991. However, Mal was being paid to lead the team and although I was happy to take over the role without receiving any payment, I wanted it to be made clear that I would not be responsible for any issues which might arise from contracts which Mal had made with other climbers on both the Everest and Lhotse expeditions. I also needed to make it clear that I needed to depart by 20 May, but until then I would do what I could to make the expedition a success. Mal had become the third veteran from the 1996 disaster to die. A tally which would keep going up over the next few years.

The following day we heard that the Indonesian team had made the first ascent of Everest that year from the Nepalese side. It later transpired that two Indonesians had climbed with their guide, the legendary Russian climber Anatoli Boukreev, and two other Russian climbers and a Sherpa, and had not reached the summit until after 3 p.m. These were the first Indonesians to reach the summit of Everest, and later reports by their

Sherpas indicated that they wouldn't have got to the top if they hadn't been dragged there by their Russian guides. Their descent back to the South Col had been made in waist-deep snow and reducing visibility, and they were very lucky to survive. Almost four weeks would pass before another successful summit was achieved on the Nepal side of the mountain.

The deaths of fellow climbers on Everest is sadly not that unusual. Of course, it has an immediate impact on climbers on the mountain, but the initial grieving process normally only lasts a short period of a few days before life on the mountain is back to normal.

I decided to rest for a few days at Base Camp, to some extent in the hope that my son Dan would arrive after his trek around Annapurna. As well as you might think you know other climbers on an expedition, there is nothing better than chatting with a family member who knows all about the nuances of your life outside of the mountains.

It was only a week after Mal's death, but the team were in good form and discussions to summit both Lhotse and Everest were taking shape. Guy Cotter was back on Everest that year, having taken over Adventure Consultants after Rob Hall's death the previous year, and we discussed the weather and the possibility that we would probably aim to go to the summit a day after Guy's team.

1 May 1997 was my forty-fifth birthday. Given that my birthday is in the middle of the pre-monsoon climbing season, I have spent a number of memorable birthdays celebrating al fresco against a wonderful mountain background, and 1997 was no exception. The Sherpa cook baked a cake and then set up a table, complete with tablecloth and serviettes, on the flat helipad which was not far from our area of Base Camp. I had brought a gourmet hamper with me from Hong Kong, which I had successfully hidden away from other climbers who may have been seeking an alternative to Base Camp rations. Although the immediate weather forecast was not encouraging, I was in good spirits and positively looking forward to the climb to the summit, which was given an extra boost when Dan arrived the next day.

It was almost exactly one year before that the teams had run into tragic difficulty by going for the summit on a pre-determined day, and all of the teams in Base Camp in early May 1997 seemed content to wait for the weather to improve before making a bid for the top of the mountain.

Mal would have been forty-four on 3 May, and I spent the day in awful weather at Base Camp.

Provisionally I planned to summit on 10 May, which would have given me just over another week on the mountain before I had to leave to fulfil other commitments. I had previously made my schedule clear to everyone when I took over the leadership, and this was not seen to be a problem given that by the stage when I needed to depart, everything would be in place for any further summit attempts. As I started up the mountain I was continuing to feel exceptionally fit, without any hint of the chest condition which had dogged me the year before, and I passed through Camp 1 after three hours and I reached Camp 2 after another two and a half hours.

I was joined later that day by another member of our team who confirmed some suspicions which I had been harbouring for a week or so. Two of our team members were husband and wife, but I had detected over the course of the expedition that a relationship had been forming between the wife and another team member, which was confirmed during the conversation at Camp 2. Such goings on are not unusual on mountaineering expeditions, but someone is always likely to get very hurt, and this would be the case later when the wife and the climber with whom she had formed a relationship told the husband in the dining tent, and in front of all the other expedition members, that they would both be leaving Base Camp to start a new life together.

On 6 May, instead of climbing up to Camp 3, I decided to take a rest day at Camp 2. It was particularly hot in my tent that afternoon and I decided to laze outside. While I lay there relaxing, at about three in the afternoon, a Sherpa was seen to fall down the Lhotse Face. His Sherpa teammates at Camp 2 immediately started to form a rescue party. Given how far he was seen to fall, there was very little chance that he had survived, but I had to remind the rescue party to take an oxygen cylinder and a mask with them before they set off towards the Lhotse Face. Sadly the Sherpa, Nima Rinzi, was already dead by the time they reached him, and his body was brought back to camp before being taken down to Base Camp.

On 7 May the weather forecast for the summit was again bad and Pete Athans, David Breashears and Guy Cotter, with whom I had been passing the time at Camp 2, decided to descend to Base Camp. I was very tempted to join them, but I had yet to climb up to Camp 3. I decided that I would try and do this the following day and, if the weather had still not cleared by then, I too would head down.

At 6 a.m. the following day I climbed alone up to Camp 3. Although the weather forecast was not good, the Malaysian team were also heading for Camp 3 with the aim of pushing on to the summit. I just hoped this would not end in disaster like the year before, but fortunately they eventually saw sense and turned back.

It was for me a very enjoyable ascent up the steep Lhotse Face to Camp 3, and I was rewarded with the Yellow Band shining out above me, and below, the Western Cwm stretching for some two kilometres from the lip of the Icefall, just beyond Camp 1. Looking down to my right were the tiny tents of Camp 2, overshadowed by the magnificence of the south-west face of Everest, first ascended almost twenty-two years before by climbers who included my good friends Peter Boardman and Pertemba Sherpa.

The weather forecast continued to look bad and I decided that there was little point remaining up on the mountain. The body of the dead Sherpa had been left at Camp 2 since his fall on 6 May, which did seem a bit odd given that had his Malaysian team members gone for the summit the day before, the body would have lain beside the tents for five days or more. Some may suggest that because he was dead it did not matter how long his body remained at Camp 2, while others would respond that the body deserved to be treated with due dignity and the priority was to get the body back to his loved ones. On the initial part of my descent on 8 May, I helped his fellow Sherpas move him across the bridges lower down in the Western Cwm before leaving them to their grim task.

I like to climb on my own wherever possible on a big mountain, as it allows me to move at my own pace whilst being responsible only to, and for, myself. Up until Mal's death I had felt very content wherever I was on the mountain and this feeling had largely continued, except for the time at Camp 2 when I found I had to sort out the quality of food, given my new position as expedition leader. It reminded me of the expedition I had led to Annapurna II and IV in 1992. That expedition included some very good climbers, with some very different egos, but everyone wanted to get to the summit. This was rather like later commercial expeditions where climbers have paid for and expect to reach the summit, and often become a group of competing individuals and pairs, rather than a cohesive team with a common goal. I was now going to discover that nothing had changed and, if anything, given the costs of climbing Everest, egos were very much going to come to the fore.

When I reached Base Camp, Brigitte Muir was the first to raise issues. This was her fourth time on Everest and she was desperate to reach the summit and claim – although she is a Belgian by birth – to become the first Australian woman to reach the top of the world. Brigitte wanted to be in the first group to next summit the mountain and wanted to use four of our Sherpas to support her, but I knew this was very contrary to what Mal had planned (and which I agreed with), which, given that we were a relatively small team, was to go for the summit after one of the larger teams on the mountain that year had opened up the route. Brigitte wasn't easily dissuaded. During the storm in 1996 she had stayed inside her tent on the South Col while the rescue took place and I very much sensed in 1997 that she was not going to let wider team considerations get in the way of her getting to the top of Everest.

It was also the day of Mal's funeral thousands of miles away in Scotland, and that evening members from all of the expeditions on the south side of Everest met at the site where we had held our team Puja ceremony only a few weeks before. It was a gathering that included most of the well-known names in 1990s Everest climbing, and Mal would have appreciated the gesture, but it also brought home again the loss of this remarkable character.

My previous sense of well-being from the time I accepted the leadership role was eroded further the following day when I had to discuss with the Mexicans their summit bid. To be fair, I had found them very good company on the mountain, but one of them, who had decided from the outset not to climb with supplementary oxygen, now wanted O2 cylinders, which he had not paid Mal for, to be placed high on the mountain just in case he needed them. Fortunately Brigitte was not around that day, having gone off with a member of another expedition, and my discussions with the Mexicans at least reached a happy conclusion. Without a leader, the expedition would have turned into chaos with everyone wanting to climb the mountain according to their own agenda and with the Sherpas stuck in the middle. I certainly wasn't being selfless when I accepted to take over from Mal, I was simply being loyal to Mal as a friend, and, having agreed to be the leader, I was not going to go back on my word. But it was becoming a pain to manage and massage the egos of a disparate group of climbers, none of whom I would have selected if I was putting together a team to climb a mountain.

We also got the news from the north side of Everest that on 7 May three Russians and a Sherpa had disappeared, and the following day, 8 May, a German climber had fallen to his death, bringing the death toll already that season to seven.

The weather forecast continued to be bad, but there was nothing to be done other than sit it out at Base Camp to wait for an improvement. The days passed and frustrated climbers aired their grievances, although there was very little that could be done to solve most issues; it was simply a case of waiting for the weather to improve.

At last there were signs that the weather was going to get better and climbers prepared themselves for the climb back up the mountain. But for me the chance of reaching the summit that year had been lost because I had to honour other commitments and I would not have the opportunity to get to the summit and back by the time I had to leave. I was of course disappointed, but certainly not distraught. The mountain would still be there next year and I knew I would be back. Like Mal, I very much enjoyed mountaineering, whether I reached summits or not. I would also be coming back to Everest while Mal would not – this was a salutary reminder that life is about lots of experiences and climbing Everest was just one of them.

Dan was still at Base Camp and he understood and supported my decision to move on, but before I did this it was essential that I made sure all was in place for the summit attempts which could still take place. Together with Kipa, our lead Sherpa, we planned what logistical support was needed to ensure that, given good weather, the other team members should be able to get safely to the summit and back. I then waited until the last possible moment before returning to Kathmandu and then on to a very different life. One of the Mexicans summitted on 23 May and Brigitte Muir reached the summit on 27 May, along with Kipa Sherpa, the last climbers to summit that season.

15

VIEW FROM THE TOP

By late 1998, a further two members of the 1996 Everest disaster had died. On 25 December 1997, while attempting the south face of Annapurna (8,091 metres) in winter, Anatoli Boukreev was swept to his death in an avalanche, having some three weeks earlier been presented with the American Alpine Club's highest award for bravery for his role during the rescue on Everest in 1996.

In 1996, the French mountaineer Chantal Mauduit successfully climbed Lhotse. Notable amongst her previous successful climbs on 8,000-metre mountains was her ascent of K2 in 1992, when she became the fourth women to reach the summit of the second highest mountain in the world. But on 11 May 1998 tragedy struck when Chantal and her Sherpa were killed in their tent when an avalanche wiped out their camp while they were climbing Dhaulagiri (8,167 metres). Tragically, of the first five women to reach the summit of K2, three died on the descent and two were later to die on other mountains.

The best combination in mountain climbing is to reach a summit and to come back safely and, of these, to come back safely is the most important. Mountaineers climb mountains to experience what life has to offer; they have a life wish, not a death wish.

On my previous two climbs on Everest I hadn't reached the top, but I wasn't perturbed. I have had the privilege to know several of the great mountaineers in recent history, including Peter Boardman, Joe Tasker and Pertemba Sherpa, but they were exceptional mountaineers who were far more capable than me and able to climb the hardest routes on Everest. I simply saw Everest and other mountains as a personal challenge rather than as a stepping-stone to fame and fortune.

In 1999, after spending the previous year exploring other mountains, I returned to Everest simply to achieve my personal ambition to reach the top. I didn't feel as fit as I had in previous years, having suffered from a herniated disc in my back caused by too much running. I had been going through a long period of treatment including being stretched on a rack once a week by a physiotherapist, but I still suffered from sciatica, the awful permanent pain which I felt down through the back of my leg. But life is short and I simply had to ignore my physical condition and I got on with getting up the mountain.

I decided to go on a trek round the Helambu valley accompanied by Karma Sherpa, the brother of Kipa, who had been our head Sherpa on my two previous expeditions to Everest, partly as a means of gaining fitness, but also to relax and to refocus on climbing big mountains in Nepal.

My aim in 1999 was to climb without any responsibility. To some extent this had also been my aim in 1996 and 1997, but events largely outside of my control had had an impact. In 1999, it was possible to buy a slot on a larger expedition's permit and I had arranged to do this through Henry Todd, who I had got to know well over the years. Henry had a very chequered past, which included being jailed in 1978 for thirteen years for drug offences. After his release from prison Henry had become an expedition organiser who specialised in organising oxygen for high altitude expeditions.

Henry had fallen foul of the Nepalese authorities and he asked me if I would become the named expedition leader, which also meant that I had to attend the pre-expedition meeting at the Nepal Ministry of Tourism, after which I would be issued with the expedition permit. As far as everyone else on the permit was concerned, particularly Henry's clients, Henry would then run the logistics of the expedition, including the organising of oxygen and the Sherpas. As far as I was concerned, I could get on with climbing Everest and, given what had happened during my previous two Everest expeditions, I was adamant that although my name was on the permit it was Henry who would be responsible for leading.

Our 1999 trek into the mountain coincided with the holding of the Everest Marathon, which starts not far from Base Camp before winding its way back to Namche Bazaar, and which at the time was held every two years. When we reached Namche Bazaar I bumped into John Bull, who had been a fellow climbing instructor with me in the army in 1975. It was a very enjoyable interlude as we caught up on what he and I had been up to over the last twenty-four years.

John was a colourful character who was taking part in the high-altitude marathon. We spent a very relaxing time en route to Base Camp reminiscing about the great times we had when we were both young instructors in Wales – including a time when John modified a canoe trailer by sawing it almost in half, which resulted in a senior army officer threatening John with a court martial.

Unusually, I chose that year to visit a local monastery on the route to seek the blessings of a lama. I am not an overly religious person, but I do believe in keeping my options open and, at $8 for the blessing and $1 for a white scarf, the ceremony seemed good value. The head lama also presented me with a small bag of rice with the instructions to throw the rice if I got caught in an avalanche – I left with great respect for his religious knowledge, but I was very sceptical about his knowledge of avalanches or how climbers should escape from them. The thought of standing firm in front of an oncoming avalanche while I searched for my bag of rice – as the avalanche moved alarmingly close – whilst still remaining calm enough to take a handful of rice from the bag and throw it in the direction of what must be by this time a wall of snow and ice, left me very unsure of the lama's wisdom.

There was an eclectic mix of climbers on the Everest permit, ranging from relatively novice climbers to professionals with a variety of reasons for being on Everest, but I had made it very clear that although I was named on the permit as the leader, it was Henry they needed to turn to for support during the next few weeks. I had simply agreed to collect the permit from the ministry in Kathmandu to avoid Henry having to continue with his problems with the government. In effect, I was an independent expedition within a larger team. I had paid for one Sherpa to climb with and I was excited about getting on again with the process of climbing the 'big hill'.

There were in effect several teams on the single climbing permit, which included Henry Todd, his clients and guide Andy Lapkass, who formed the Himalayan Guides team, and three independent expeditions formed by the Mexican mountaineer Elsa Carsolio, fellow Briton Graham Ratcliffe, and me. Henry's team also included Ray Brown from New Zealand, the immensely strong American climber Dr Lauri Medina, who I had climbed with in Tibet the year before, and the British climber Dave Mellor, who was an immediately likeable character, having been part of the strong generation of British rock climbers of the 1960s.

The scene was almost set for what was going to become a highly controversial season, but there was also one other team who would play a prominent part as the season progressed. This was the Out There Trekking (OTT) team led by Jon Tinker, who in 1993 had become the first British climber to reach the summit of Everest from Tibet, and guided by Nick Kekus, an intelligent and immensely strong professional guide who had reached the summit of Everest in 1997.

The season started like any other season on Everest. Climbers took their first steps into the Icefall and the acclimatisation process began. On our first climb through the Icefall I was largely on my own, although at the top I met the legendary Babu Sherpa, who had previously been the sirdar for OTT and was planning to sleep overnight on top of Everest later that season without oxygen. Babu was very strong, like all of the Sherpas, but unlike the others he was actually a bit podgy. Climbers on Everest burn about twice as many calories per day as they would during an average day at sea level. In addition, altitude often depresses a climber's appetite, and the result is that calories are difficult to replace and during weeks on the mountain climbers lose a large amount of weight. The theory is for climbers to

arrive at the mountain 'fat and fit', however, I don't think Babu ever sub-
scribed to this theory – he was simply always 'amazingly fit, while being
a bit fat'.

During my initial stay at Camp 1 I yet again came down with a bad
stomach, but I managed to sort this out and continued to climb up to
Camp 2. Although this was on 17 April, the conversations about summit
attempts were already beginning. To some extent I believe the discussions
reflected the fact that there were four climbers on the mountain that year
who could become the first British mountaineer to twice reach the summit
of Everest: Jon Tinker, Nick Kekus, and Mike Smith, who were all climbing
with OTT, and Graham Ratcliffe, who was climbing independently, but
supported by Himalayan Guides.

I got the impression over the next couple of days at Camp 2 that there
were competing forces at play which meant that a two-speed strategy for
climbing the mountain was emerging. A number of climbers were seeking
an early summit. Graham Ratcliffe, for example, had already slept at
Camp 3, which is normally the signal that a climber is ready for the summit,
but there were also other climbers from other nations who were vying to
be the first from their various countries to reach the summit of Everest.

In 1999, climbers on commercial expeditions seemed to be paying
upwards of $40,000 to be part of a team. More often than not, the first time
a commercial expedition would meet with clients was when they arrived
in Kathmandu en route to the mountain. This was not a problem for
climbers who had the necessary experience to be on Everest, but for a few
this meant that their first climb through the Icefall would be a test to
determine whether or not they should continue to climb higher on the
mountain. It was an annual test that not everyone passed, and already a
Guatemalan had left Base Camp having failed to climb through the Icefall;
in effect he had wasted over $40,000 by simply not being up to the challenge.
This was yet another example of a moral issue which was becoming a
problem on the mountain. Some commercial expedition companies were

accepting clients with totally inadequate climbing experience, knowing full well that the client was unlikely to make it through the Icefall, and in the process these companies were happy to make thousands of dollars in profit.

My good friend Pertemba Sherpa was managing a Japanese team, and during my time at Base Camp we often chatted. I also spent time relaxing when not on the mountain by dining with my friends Jon Tinker and Nick Kekus at the OTT camp.

My climbing partner in 1999 was Pasang Dawa, a fit young Sherpa with a wry sense of humour. I particularly enjoyed spending time with Pasang Dawa because it gave me an opportunity to speak the language which I had first learnt almost twenty-five years before when I joined the Gurkhas. Nepali is a honorific language, with speakers using different verb forms depending on the status of other people in the conversation. On long expeditions over the years I had spent too much time conversing with Sherpas, and the polished form of the language which I had learned on the British Army Gurkhali language course had been replaced by a more coarse form of speech – in effect I had now learned to speak the language like a peasant.

It is virtually impossible to isolate oneself from the politics and team squabbles which are a fixture of the Everest season, not the least because I was relying on Himalayan Guides to provide me with food and tents, which meant I regularly camped and ate with them while on the mountain. As always, there was plenty of time spent at camps 1 and 2 during the acclimatisation phase, and inevitably climbers visited other team's camps to pass the time.

The sheer financial cost of climbing Everest means that many climbers increasingly expose their selfish nature as the season develops and the opportunities to go for the summit start to appear. Climbers have paid vast sums of money to be on the mountain and they all expect a shot at the summit. Add to this the fact that high altitude climbers have to be strong willed, and you get all the ingredients for the mountain equivalent of a bar room brawl. Fights are fortunately rare but they do happen. However, daily shouting matches are more common, and nothing in a tented camp can be kept private.

Henry Todd had for a number of years been responsible for supplying oxygen to a number of the teams climbing Everest and, historically, Henry had provided oxygen cylinders constructed and filled by the Russian Poisk company. However, by 1999 he decided that it would be easier to supply oxygen cylinders which had been made in the UK and filled in India. A large number of teams on Everest had contracts with Henry that year for him to supply them with oxygen, but it was not widely known that these would be from the UK rather than from the Poisk factory – I had certainly never been made aware of this.

I personally would have had a problem had I known where the oxygen was being filled. In the early 1980s, while I was staying at the Gurkha camp in Dharan in eastern Nepal, which had its own British military hospital, I had been asked by a friend who was an army surgeon to take photographs of an operation he was particularly keen to record. The patient, who was about ten years old, had been born with the middle fingers of both hands joined together, and the unique, but apparently straightforward, operation would separate the fingers.

The patient was anaesthetised and all seemed to be going well until my friend the surgeon tried to take skin from the young boy's buttocks to be grafted onto the fingers. As the skin was shaved off, blood should have appeared – but there was none, and despite a frantic effort to revive the boy, he was declared dead. A tragic end to what should have been a simple operation.

A few months later I learned that around this time there had been other deaths during operations at Dharan and the British military police had been called in to investigate. They soon discovered that the gas bottles supplied from India for use by the anaesthetist during the operations had not been filled with oxygen, but had instead been filled with a lethal gas in order to allow the supplier in India to make a greater profit.

In addition to supplying climbing expeditions, Henry had previously discussed with me a plan to approach the Indian government to try and sell them oxygen systems to be used by their soldiers who were based high in the Himalaya, facing the Pakistan army. Henry felt that his time spent in prison would be discovered by the Indians, but my time as an officer in the Gurkhas would allow me to make a credible approach to the Indian government. I did not see myself as a salesman of oxygen, or anything else, and I declined to be involved.

Whilst I had been at Base Camp I had noticed that Andy Lapkass and Henry had spent a lot of time in the tent where the oxygen systems were stored. There had also been some rumours circulating for some days about oxygen issues, but it wasn't until 30 April that I became fully aware of the problem. On that day as I lay in my tent at Camp 2, I heard Andy Lapkass, the guide for Henry's Himalayan Guides, having a heated discussion with someone whose voice I didn't recognise. I got up and confronted Andy and at last he admitted there was a problem. When the cylinders arrived at Base Camp it had been found that the thread on the neck of the British bottles was too long – when the connector was screwed on to the bottle, the pin in the connector could not reach the valve seated in the neck, which opened the valve which controlled the flow of the oxygen.

I was astonished. Clearly this issue had been known for some time, but instead of letting the climbers who were going to be using the oxygen system know about the problem, both Henry and Andy had decided to keep this information to themselves. It later transpired that they had gradually told some of the leaders of the large expeditions to whom they were supplying with oxygen, but there had been a tacit agreement not to spread the news.

The situation was ludicrous. Of course, some people climb Everest without the use of supplementary oxygen, but the vast majority use it, not just to enable them to reach the summit, but more importantly to ensure that they reach the summit and descend safely.

One solution being tried was to file the thread down to a size where it allowed the pin to open the valve. But this had to be an accurate procedure, because if the thread was filed down too much, the pin would then overly press against the valve and bend when the adaptor was screwed on to the bottle. It would have been difficult enough to adapt the large number of problem cylinders in a workshop, and on the mountain the best place to carry out this work would have been at Base Camp. It was grossly irresponsible to distribute cylinders to different camps on the mountain where the work to file down the thread was going to be far more problematic – and this is exactly what happened with many of the cylinders.

Even more bizarre was the second solution being proposed to solve the problem. This was to balance a small polystyrene ball on the valve head in the neck of the bottle to bridge the gap between the valve head and the pin when the connector was screwed on to the bottle. This was a preposterous solution because the adaptor couldn't be removed once the polystyrene ball had been locked in place and it would have meant that there needed to be an equal number of adaptors and cylinders, which there wasn't. It also didn't take account of the fundamental need to change cylinders on the way to the summit. The thought of climbers wearing large protective mittens attempting to balance a small polystyrene ball on a valve, possibly in the dark, but also very possibly in high wind, was ludicrous.

Larger teams in particular were starting to panic. OTT for example had clients paying at least $40,000, but they also had a team within a team who were paying far more. The Greek multimillionaire Constantine 'Cos' Niarchos was aiming to become the first climber from his country to reach the summit of Everest and he was employing his own guide and Sherpas to do this.

I was very fond of Cos, having climbed with him the previous year. He had had some problems with drugs as he grew up, which he had overcome, and he had become a competent mountaineer. I certainly didn't have a problem that he had paid for extra support on Everest; he had the money to do this and it seemed perfectly sensible and it shouldn't have impacted on other climbers, many of whom would have done the same had they been able to afford it.

The problem now, for everyone who had a contract to use the oxygen, was that there was no Plan B. For them, and this included me, the only available options were to use the modified British bottles or to abandon the climb and leave the mountain.

Everest climbers are often accused of being selfish in their attempts to climb the mountain and there have been examples, particularly on the Tibetan side of the mountain, when climbers have refused to stop to help others who are having problems because this would have meant them giving up their own summit attempts. This selfish attitude now started to become apparent once again because, whilst there were a large number of problem cylinders, there were also some perfectly serviceable Poisk cylinders available in the stockpiles at different camps, and climbers were starting to squabble about who was going to get the Poisk bottles.

It was easier for me to deal with this crisis than it was for others. I didn't have any clients to worry about and, although I made my thoughts known about the incompetent way the provision of oxygen was being managed, I simply got on with the process of preparing myself for a summit attempt.

1 May 1999 was my forty-seventh birthday and again I was celebrating the occasion on a mountain. I was still considering leaving that day for Camp 3, and then the summit, and I would take my chances with the oxygen systems which I found when I arrived at Camp 4. However, the weather forecast appeared to indicate that it would be better to go for 4 May and I delayed my departure from Camp 2. I subsequently recon-sidered this plan when I saw how many climbers were arriving at Camp 2 en route to the summit. My plan was simply to climb with Pasang Dawa, and although this would in all likelihood be with other climbers on the route, I saw no point in climbing in the midst of the large numbers who were now heading for the summit.

It wasn't just the large number of climbers which was giving me concern. There were also several incompetent climbers amongst the group who shouldn't have been on the mountain that year, and two of them in particular had given me some concern whenever I watched them on the mountain. When they arrived at camp on 2 May, having taken twice the average time to climb from Base Camp, I decided that it would be prudent to wait for a second favourable forecast before going for the summit.

That day we also received the news that a good friend, Michael Jorgensen, had been killed while climbing on Makalu. This was very sad for all of us who knew him, but it had a particular impact on one of Henry's Sherpas because Michael was supporting his son through school.

I stayed at Camp 2 on 3 May while I watched over sixty climbers ascend the Lhotse Face. The weather deteriorated later that day and I heard on the radio that the leader of the OTT team, Jon Tinker, had a problem.

Jon was a straight-talking, experienced mountaineer who I had grown to like. He stood no nonsense during conversations if he felt he was in the right, and he could appear unfriendly on occasions, but once you got to know him as a friend, one found a kind and generous personality. Although Jon had been many times to altitude, including the summit of Everest in 1993, which he climbed with Babu Sherpa, he had suffered a minor stroke.

Most of the OTT team decided to descend the mountain with Jon, and all of them except for the young British climber Mike Matthews and the Canadian climber Dave Rodney returned to Base Camp.

Mike Matthews was an extremely likeable twenty-three-year-old who was intelligent and great company to be with. He was the same age as my son Dan and I had always enjoyed Mike's company whenever we met on the mountain. Conversely, Dave Rodney seemed to have a very high opinion of himself and I never found his company enjoyable. I had first seen him on the flight into Kathmandu from Bangkok when I could not get over how long he spent combing his hair as he moved around the cabin – a slightly bizarre observation, but it was significant enough for me to make a comment in my diary before I later found out that he was on an Everest team.

Rodney in particular was not happy that the OTT team had descended with Jon Tinker, and eventually he had to be 'ordered' back down to Base Camp.

Whilst no one went to the summit on the morning of 4 May, Andy Lapkass was now at the South Col with most of the Himalayan Guides team ready for a summit attempt on 5 May. In the meantime, I had decided after ten nights at Camp 2 to descend to Base Camp to rest before my own attempt on the summit.

It is always exciting when teams start to attempt to summit Everest, and I was awake early on the morning of 5 May to see how the Himalayan Guides team were progressing up the mountain. At 10.30 a.m. we heard that Pete Athans had reached the summit of Everest for the sixth time and, later, Andy Lapkass, Ray Brown, Elsa Carsolio and Graham Ratcliffe (becoming the first British climber to summit Everest twice) had joined him there.

What was alarming, however, was that Lauri Medina had fallen when a cornice had collapsed while on the section between the South Summit and the Hillary Step. Fortunately she had been attached to a fixed rope, but she had still been dangling in space before being rescued, after which she returned to the South Col. Andy and the other summiteers took an abnormally long time to descend to the South Col, but by 7 p.m. we knew that they were all safely back at camp.

The following day Lauri was suffering with snow blindness and decided to stay with Andy Lapkass at the South Col for another day, while Graham, Ray and Elsa descended to Camp 2.

The weather forecast for the coming days didn't look brilliant, but I was ready to go for the summit and I forced myself to relax and to be patient – which was not easy because I found myself getting very irritated by a very noisy trekker who had decided to pitch a tent next to mine at Base Camp.

Elsa arrived back in Base Camp on Friday 7 May and looked in great shape. Over a cup of coffee she told me about Lauri's fall from the ridge above the South Summit. After the cornice had given way, Lauri had fallen about seven metres and was dangling in space above a sheer drop of thousands of feet. Elsa was above her on the ridge and she was relieved to see what she thought was another climber coming towards them with a rope to rescue Lauri. But when the climber reached Elsa he continued to pass by saying that he was taking the rope to Pete Athans who was further up the ridge fixing the Hillary Step, without any thought for Lauri, who was in danger and urgently needed a rope to be rescued. Fortunately other climbers then arrived to recover Lauri.

Elsa then went on to say that when they had all descended to the South Col they found that the only two sleeping bags which were available were being used by other team members and Lauri and Elsa were forced to spend the night wearing only their down clothing.

Graham Ratcliffe had succeeded in becoming the first British climber to twice reach the summit of Everest, for which I congratulated him when he returned to Base, but I did feel a comment he made that, 'Jon Tinker would have killed himself trying to beat me' was inappropriate and I told him so. I knew Jon well enough to know that he wasn't interested in meaningless records and was instead more concerned about the welfare of his team.

I had decided to spend one more day at Base Camp before my summit attempt, which now looked like it would be on 12 May 1999 – what would have been my grandmother's one-hundredth birthday, which I hoped was going to be a good omen. After breakfast I walked over to the bottom of the Icefall to welcome back Lauri and Andy. Lauri seemed to have got over her bout of snow blindness but, most importantly, it was good to see her safely back at Base Camp. Babu Sherpa also returned that day after spending twenty hours on the summit of Everest without oxygen – a tremendous feat of survival by a Sherpa legend, even if it did seem rather pointless.

I had dinner with Pete Athans that night, a great person and climber, and a very competent Nepali speaker. I had developed the greatest respect for Pete over the years and his wish for a safe and successful climb was gratefully received.

16

THE SUMMIT AT LAST

It snowed very heavily that night, which I thought was not the best omen for the climb ahead. It would have been nice to stay in my sleeping bag, given how warm it was inside my tent and how bloody miserable I knew it would be outside. But staying there was not going to get me up the mountain. I got up at 4 a.m., an hour or so earlier than I normally did for a climb through the Icefall, but I wanted very much to start the journey into the Icefall from Base Camp.

Walking through Base Camp is always difficult in the pre-dawn darkness, particularly after a heavy snowfall. The normal paths had disappeared and, much to the annoyance of climbers who were trying to sleep, I kept tripping over tent guy ropes. The snow had also settled on the prayer flags which were strung all over Base Camp, weighing them down, so I had to continually lift them over my head in order to pass by, getting an extremely wet and cold handful of snow down the back of my neck in the process.

Not only was it difficult to navigate through Base Camp, but the Icefall was also covered in deep snow and, although I love being on my own in such an awe-inspiring environment, I was regretting that I had left before the Sherpas, who had opened the trail and were far more familiar with the route than I was. The trail in parts was only marked by wands and I guessed where the route between each wand ran, frequently getting it wrong and ending up putting my feet into pools of freezing water which were hidden under the snow and a thin layer of ice. At least the occasional section of fixed rope kept me going in the right direction.

Just before the first long jumar, Sherpas appeared out of the dark from behind me and with good nature they berated me for breaking trail on my own as they zoomed off into the darkness ahead. Nick Kekus also caught up with me and slowed down to climb with me as the sun rose and we moved on to the top of the Icefall.

Nick is an exceptional mountaineer and good friend and it was a pleasure to climb with him. After Jon Tinker's departure following his stroke, Nick had taken over leadership of the OTT team who were also making their way back up the mountain.

It may have been my early efforts in the Icefall before the sun rose which made me feel unusually tired when we reached Camp 1, or it may have been due to the blow to my morale caused by the unexpected heavy snowfall overnight. Whatever the cause of the tiredness, I needed to rest for a while before continuing up through the Western Cwm to Camp 2.

The cold, miserable weather had been bad enough, but the weather then completely changed and it became unbearably hot – in all the times I had climbed through the cwm this was the least enjoyable, and it didn't bode well for my summit attempt.

There was no point in continuing up to Camp 3 the following day. I needed to get my strength back. Fortunately, because it was just Pasang Dawa and me going together to the summit, we were very flexible, and adding another day into our programme was not a problem. I managed to spend the day relaxing at camp and I recovered quickly from the exertions of the previous day. Nick came over from the OTT camp to see how I was and it now looked as if we would all be going for the summit at the same time on 13 May.

Henry Todd was also running a Lhotse team in 1999, whom I had had nothing to do with until we ended up at Camp 2 together on 9 May. On the morning of 11 May, Henry sent them a very bizarre message telling them to go immediately to Camp 3, which was shared by both Everest and Lhotse teams, and for them to then go to their Camp 4 which should have been on the Lhotse Face at a point directly down from the summit of Lhotse. But this Camp 4 didn't exist and, as I moved off from Camp 2 at 10 a.m.,

I left behind a very irritated and increasingly uncooperative Lhotse team, who were having a very angry discussion with Henry on the radio. It was with a great deal of relief that I moved upwards.

The plan was for me to move up to Camp 3 where I would spend the night. In the meantime, Pasang Dawa would move to Camp 2. We would both then climb to Camp 4 the following day, together with a support Sherpa who would cook for us and wait for us at the South Col while we made our summit attempt.

I had my strength back and it was a very relaxing climb up the Lhotse Face to Camp 3, where I occupied a tent and afterwards continued to brew hot drinks and relax throughout the day. I used half a bottle of oxygen on a low flow-rate to help me rest – the system worked well and there was as yet no sign that oxygen was as big a problem as we thought it would be almost two weeks before.

On the radio that evening I heard the discussions between Henry Todd and his Lhotse team, who had refused to follow his directions, and were firmly staying put at Camp 2.

It is another example of how much fitter Sherpas are than the other climbers on Everest that on their way to the summit they climb directly from Camp 2 to the South Col, missing out the need to sleep at Camp 3. I was woken early on the morning of 12 May by Sherpas passing my tent. I put my head out of the tent to say hello, only to receive good-natured abuse for still being in my sleeping bag.

It had been a cold night and I wasn't in any particular hurry to start the climb to the col, but I eventually forced my way upwards at 9 a.m. It is an easy, steady climb up the face and across to the Yellow Band, but this was the first time during this expedition that I had been to that altitude and I was certainly feeling the lack of oxygen in the air.

The Yellow Band is a relatively low cliff, which is easily climbed with the aid of fixed ropes. While I was taking a short rest there I met three Mexican friends, Luis, Carlos and Hugo who were descending after an unsuccessful summit attempt. They had gone for the summit on 11 May and had been forced to turn around close to the Balcony, about one third of the way up the south-east ridge from the South Col. These were three strong climbers, but they were also sensible, and they would be back for another attempt at the summit.

From the Yellow Band the route climbed gradually up to the Geneva Spur, from where the route steepens until the top of the spur, from where it is an easy walk into the South Col.

It wouldn't be unfair to describe the South Col as the most miserable campsite in the world. It is barren and very cold, with almost a constant wind as the air is forced through the gap caused by Everest on one side and Lhotse on the other.

The idea is to arrive at Camp 4 and to then rest up during the remainder of that day before leaving for the summit around midnight. The Balcony is normally reached at about 4 a.m. as the sun starts to appear over the horizon, then it is a steep climb up the south-east ridge to reach the South Summit at about 7 a.m. Then the route takes the knife-edge leading up to the Hillary Step, after which it is a relatively easy walk to the summit, which is normally reached at about 9.30 a.m. This then allows for a significant amount of daylight during which climbers can safely return to the South Col. If climbers are late for any reason and fail to reach the summit by noon, there is an unwritten rule that they should turn round and start to descend. What had happened almost three years earlier to the day, when some climbers were still going for the summit late into the afternoon, was still very fresh in my memory.

I arrived at the South Col at 2.30 p.m. feeling very dehydrated, but there was no sign of Pasang Dawa or our support Sherpa, Pemba. Fortunately OTT's Martin Doyle and Mike Matthews very kindly asked me to join them in their tent to shelter and to share a brew. Martin was a very experienced guide who exuded competence. Mike was simply a charming young man of whom any parent would have been proud. They both seemed in very good form and we idled away the time while I waited for Pasang Dawa and Pemba to arrive, which they did not long afterwards.

I was still feeling desperately dehydrated, but after joining Pasang Dawa and Pemba it took a very long time to produce a drink and by this time we only had about three and a half hours before we had to leave for the summit. I was continuing to feel very thirsty and increasingly tired.

Even if climbers manage to sleep at Camp 2 on their way to the summit and back, there is very little opportunity for sleep at camps 3 and 4, and any climber who reaches the summit of Everest has probably gone without useful sleep for some sixty hours at some stage during the process.

I lay in my sleeping bag until at about 10 p.m. from the various tents across the col came the sounds of climbers stirring and preparing to start the climb to the summit. We did the same and Pasang Dawa and I started our climb at 11 p.m.

Climbing at that altitude is not comfortable. The large down jackets and trousers make each movement feel clumsy. The oxygen mask, goggles and all-over face covering significantly limit the climber's vision, which is in any case restricted to the small area illuminated by the head torch. It is vitally important to ensure that there is no exposed skin which could be affected by frostbite during the night or by the intense ultraviolet rays which exist in the atmosphere at that altitude during the day time.

Another complication is the need to wear large gloves, which are generally not needed lower down the mountain. These gloves make it very difficult to hold the ice axe and to open and close karabiners at the cross-over points on the fixed ropes. I was very grateful when Pasang Dawa worked with me at the cross-over points – there was no room for pride, we were in this together.

In the pitch-blackness between the South Col and the Balcony there was little point in trying to overtake or manoeuvre for position in what was then becoming a group of some twenty-five climbers going for the summit that night. There were frequent rests while whoever was at the front of the line sorted the route out, and I had no idea of time or distance, simply that we were gradually moving upwards. I longed to reach the Balcony and the onset of daybreak so that I could start to have an appreciation of the progress we were making.

About 3 a.m. we passed the Balcony, but I was still not sure of our exact progress until suddenly the sky lightened with the onset of a magnificent sunrise. In normal circumstances, and at another point of the earth's surface, I would have stopped and bathed in its awesome beauty, but I was attempting to reach the highest point in the world and I just moved on and on.

Some way up the steepening south-east ridge above the Balcony, Pasang Dawa and I tried to change my oxygen bottle which I didn't think was working well or at all. We had previously tested the regulator, which was attached to a British oxygen bottle, but it clearly wasn't working. Pasang Dawa then suggested we turned round, which in my oxygen-starved state I at first agreed with, followed very quickly by me bluntly stating that there was no way this was going to cause me to turn around. Pasang Dawa then gave me a Poisk bottle to try and I started to move on upwards again.

For some reason, perhaps because there was a problem with his oxygen, a little further up the ridge Dave Rodney from the OTT group was wandering off the route and had to be strongly told to get back on the climbing path, given that a slight slip would see him plummet down into Tibet.

The south-east ridge never loses its steepness – on and on we climbed. It is difficult to have a clear idea of what was happening to the other climbers, given that the line was now spread out and Pasang Dawa and I were moving nearer to the front of the group.

The oxygen leaking up from my face mask continually fogged up my glasses and having to frequently stop to clear them was becoming irritating. At least this was becoming a little easier because I was able to take off my outer gloves as the temperature had gradually increased since sunrise. There was a point at about 6 a.m., when I was still an hour below the South

Summit, when I became confident that I was going to reach the top – it had taken a significant effort to get that far which I wasn't prepared to waste.

Climbing just in front of me as we approached the South Summit was the very strong Dutch woman, Katja Staartjes, who was part of the OTT team. Ahead of us we could see two snow features which later turned out to be false summits on the south-east ridge but, from where we were, Katja thought it might be the summit and she asked me how far we had to go. I held up two fingers to indicate two hours, but Katja kept asking the same question until I realised that my two fingers were covered by my inner mitten and Katja had no idea what I was trying to indicate. I then held up my two thumbs which seemed to satisfactorily answer Katja's question.

This is just one example of the impact of altitude and how difficult it is to think clearly the higher a climber gets on the mountain. Unlike divers in the sea, who rely completely on their breathing apparatus, climbers only use supplementary oxygen – in effect, a normal breath is taken through the front of the mask while at the same time a whiff of oxygen is added to that breath from the cylinder through the mask. This means that climbers can use far smaller cylinders and for far longer than divers under the sea.

We reached the South Summit at 7 a.m. and I clearly remembered that this was where Rob Hall had been when he made his last radio messages in 1996. This was also the point which was reached by John Hunt's first summit pair in 1953, the British climbers Charles Evans and Tom Bourdillon. They got there late in the day with no idea whether or not the ridge or cliff ahead of them was climbable. Three days later, on 29 May 1953, Ed Hillary and Tenzing Norgay reached the summit and, since then, by 1999, over 900 individual climbers had followed them to the summit from both Tibet and Nepal.

Those first climbers on the mountain had been very courageous, with equipment far inferior to that which we were to use in later years. They didn't even know if it was possible to reach the summit and to return safely.

How much easier it was for the rest of us who were merely following in their footsteps.

The ridge from the South Summit is steep and narrow as it snakes upwards to the Hillary Step. Although not technically difficult, it can be very dangerous and Lauri's fall through the cornice only a few days before was certainly on my mind.

Ahead of me on the ridge I counted twelve climbers, which surprised me given that this meant we were in the middle of the group that had left the South Col last night. It later transpired that nine of the twelve were Sherpas, who for some reason had gone ahead of their teams, most of whom were still behind us and below the south summit.

It didn't take long to climb the knife-edge ridge or to climb the Hillary Step, which simply turned out to be a quick heave up some fixed ropes – how very different it must have been when Ed Hillary first forced his way up this cliff.

Some days later, when I wrote in my diary, I couldn't remember how long it took me to walk over the snow slope above the Hillary Step to reach the summit. I wrote that I thought it took twenty minutes before, at last, there in front of me was the highest point in the world. As well as a group of Sherpas, ahead of me on the summit were Cos Niarchos and his guide Augusto Ortega, and the Japanese climber Ken Noguchi.

The summit of Everest is formed by a small, snow-covered crest which runs at right angles to the route from the Nepalese side. At last, after three expeditions to Everest, I had reached this point. I felt the greatest excitement when I was only twenty metres from the summit and I knew that nothing was going to stop me getting there. I was also aware that most climbers die on the descent and I was conscious that the climb was still far from complete.

17

MOST CLIMBERS DIE DURING THE DESCENT

I took some photos, including one of a banner in support of saving my local hospital back in Gosport in the UK. I also had a photo with Cos and Pasang Dawa before we started our descent. We had arrived at 9.26 a.m. and we left at 9.45 a.m. The weather at the summit was fine, but there was a disturbing amount of cloud bubbling up below us and I was again reminded of what had happened in 1996.

Katja and Dave Rodney had reached the summit not long after Pasang Dawa and me, and on the descent, just before we reached the Hillary Step, we passed Chris Brown and Martin Doyle. I had a little epic at the Hillary Step, which I decided to descend using my figure-of-8 descender, which I dropped while I was trying to attach it to a rope, but an Italian hitch through my karabiner worked just as well.

It is not always easy to recognise climbers, given we are wearing full down suits with our faces hidden behind oxygen masks, and I didn't realise at the time that the climber I passed at the bottom of the Hillary Step was Mike Matthews.

Not long after passing Mike I met Nick Kekus, who was sitting down in the snow. I thought initially that he was a Sherpa until a voice asked, 'Is that you Mike?' In my view Nick was doing a first-class job in leading his team that day; he could have easily become the second British climber to twice reach the summit, but such records were of no interest to Nick. Instead he positioned himself to ensure climbers were appropriately supported by other guides and Sherpas.

We changed oxygen cylinders again at the South Summit, but it became apparent very quickly that yet again mine wasn't working. There was little point in trying to sort it out and I told Pasang Dawa to keep heading down and I would follow. What shocked me was just how quickly I became very tired as we descended the south-east ridge. I soon became absolutely exhausted and I kept on sitting down. Fortunately, it was still very early in the day, about noon, and I had plenty of time to reach the South Col in daylight. I could only imagine how the climbers who had summited in 1996 had felt when they started to run out of oxygen while they descended in a storm and with limited visibility, having reached the summit late in the afternoon.

Not far below the Balcony there was a sudden whoosh and an oxygen cylinder flew past me at head height and almost hit Ken Noguchi, who was just below me. There is no doubt that either of us would have been killed if it had hit us. I was annoyed that someone was clumsy enough further up the mountain to kick it loose without giving a warning to those below but, to be fair, we were by this time far below others on the route and I probably wouldn't have heard a warning even if one had been shouted.

As I descended to the South Col, I didn't appreciate in my exhausted state just how much the weather had deteriorated. We had noticed the bubbling clouds when we had looked down from the summit, but I hadn't thought at all about the weather since then – I was solely focused on getting my body, which was becoming difficult to move, down to the sanctuary of Camp 4. I only realised just how bad conditions were when I returned home and saw a photograph I had taken just after the near miss incident with the oxygen cylinder, which showed that developing cloud had severely restricted the visibility as we approached our top camp.

At last we reached the South Col at 2.30 p.m. and crawled into our tent, where we lay in an exhausted state while Pemba helped us out of our climbing equipment, before we spent the rest of the afternoon resting and taking in fluids.

As it got dark we heard a metallic clanging sound outside our tent and Pasang Dawa said that he thought some climbers had still not made it back to camp and the noise being made was to guide them in to the South Col.

We had some old oxygen cylinders which Pemba had found while we had been making our summit attempt, and, although they were only partially full, they at least worked and we used them as we dozed fitfully through the night. As we lay there after sunrise the following morning, trying to get our bodies to move to prepare ourselves to depart, Nick Kekus arrived at our tent. Before Nick spoke I knew he was going to tell me that something bad had happened. My immediate thought was that he had heard on his radio some terrible news to tell me about my children in the UK, which was in retrospect a completely irrational thought, but I can still clearly recall that feeling of dread.

Mike Matthews, the charming and intelligent young man who I had got to know well during the expedition, and who I had shared a brew with when I reached the South Col less than forty-eight hours before, had not made it back to the camp the night before.

I felt devastated and my immediate thoughts were for his parents. He was almost certainly dead and they would have to go through the ordeal that all parents fear: to be told that their child has died.

The previous day Mike had reached the summit at around noon, together with the guide Mike Smith who had just become the second British climber to reach the summit more than once. There were no Sherpas with them and they then started to descend and had reached a point below the Hillary Step by 1 p.m., and the South Summit by 2 p.m., which should still have given them plenty of daylight in which to descend. They then headed down, with Mike Smith going ahead to free the ropes, in what must have been rapidly worsening weather, considering what we were experiencing lower down at the same time.

At some stage during the descent to the Balcony, the two climbers lost contact with each other and, although Mike Smith waited at the Balcony, Mike Matthews was never seen again. Already frostbitten, Mike Smith was eventually forced to move on down to Camp 4.

I felt numb. Death on high mountains is certainly not rare, but the comparison between Mike and my children led me straightaway to ponder whether or not climbing Everest was worth the cost of a young life.

Later that day, Jon Tinker, who was by then back in the UK and had been given the news from Base Camp, phoned the Matthews family to tell them that Mike had been missing for twenty hours.

I later made my way off the South Col in what was still very gloomy weather. I overtook Martin Doyle on my way to the Geneva Spur and we silently looked at each other, our expressions showing the grief we felt. At the Yellow Band I lost my spare figure-of-8 descender, which was an odd repetition of the incident at the Hillary Step the day before. Further down, as I approached Camp 3, the weather turned particularly nasty and it was a slow, miserable journey to reach Camp 2.

I reached Camp 2 at 12.30 p.m., but before any of those at camp could start to congratulate me I told them about what I knew of Mike's disappearance the day before. There was nothing to feel triumphant about; a young life had been lost. The weather at Camp 2 was awful that afternoon and I stayed in my small tent with my own thoughts, while other team members worked to stop the dining tent from being blown away.

It normally takes a couple of days to descend from Camp 4 to Base Camp after a summit bid, and often longer in the sort of weather we were experiencing, but I simply wanted to get down and off the mountain. I left Camp 2 on Saturday 15 May and trudged through heavy snow down the Western Cwm to Camp 1. It was far more dangerous than I had previously experienced in the cwm, with crevasses hidden by the snow, and slippery, unstable ladders bridging across the known ones.

The Icefall was even worse, and although I had started down from Camp 2 fairly late, I was the first person that day to descend through the Icefall until some Sherpas overtook me in the middle section. Over the years I had been through the Icefall on about thirty occasions, but this was by far the worst trip. The snow had changed everything.

Perhaps the need to focus during the journey down had calmed my spirit.

I still felt sad, but the heavy grief which I had experienced higher on the mountain had lifted somewhat by the time I reached Base Camp. One of the first to congratulate me was Pertemba Sherpa, which meant a lot. He presented me with the first of many white scarves which I would collect on the way back to Kathmandu. I was keen to phone the news of my summit success through to my children in the UK but, of course, such is the modern world: they had already read about it on the internet. That night I had a solemn dinner with Nick, Lauri and Chris Brown and, after going to bed at 8 p.m., I had my first reasonable night of sleep in several days.

For those left on the mountain there was still an issue about oxygen and there were no further successful summits until 26 May when eleven climbers reached the top.

A week after climbing Everest I was at Lukla waiting for a flight back to Kathmandu, desperate to get home to see my family and then to see what other challenges life would have waiting for me.

On arrival back in the UK it was important for me to see my children. I went first to see my son, Tom, followed by my daughter Nicole at the final speech day at her school in Cranbrook in Kent. Then, on 4 June, I travelled with my son Dan from Durham University, where he was studying, to the home of Chris Brown, who had reached the summit of Everest shortly after I did on 13 May, thus completing his quest to climb the seven summits. Also at this mini Everest reunion was Jon Tinker, the first Briton to climb the mountain from the Tibetan side, and Nick Kekus, who reached the summit in 1997.

When I arrived, Chris immediately asked me if I had heard the news. In a sport where deaths occur regularly, I knew straight away that someone I knew had died. But when Chris showed me a newspaper clipping I was surprised and shocked. Cos Niarchos had died at his London home on

31 May, eighteen days after reaching the summit just before me. Apparently he had suffered a heart attack.

It did not seem possible that someone who could reach the summit of Everest could die so soon afterwards in such a way. We speculated that Cos's rapid descent, aided by the change of pressure during the helicopter flight he used to immediately fly back to Kathmandu after reaching Base Camp, may have brought on the attack, but none of us had heard of such a thing happening before.

The funeral took place in Switzerland the following week and his team members Jon, Nick and Chris were among the mourners. His family had placed a photograph of Cos on the summit of Everest on his coffin, and they asked Nick to identify the climber next to him. When Nick told them that it was me and I was going to be at my farmhouse in Normandy the following week, they passed a message to me, inviting me to meet at their stud farm, which coincidentally turned out to be only a short drive from my French house. It immediately became clear when I visited his family that Cos and I lived very different lifestyles when his extraordinarily wealthy sister, having heard that my house wasn't far away, asked me if I also bred horses. I was, however, happy to chat about being with Cos when he had achieved his ambition to become the first Greek climber to reach the summit of Everest.

On 7 July an inquest into Cos's death was held in London and next day the newspapers recorded that he had died from an enormous cocaine overdose – he had taken several times the amount of cocaine normally associated with drug-related deaths. The pathologist at the inquest also reported that Cos had a degree of heart disease, which could have caused his death at any time, although there had been no heart attack.

Cos was born Constantine Niarchos, the fourth son of the 'Golden Greek' Stavros Niarchos, the billionaire shipping rival of Aristotle Onassis. During his time at Harrow, one of Britain's top public schools, Cos received £500 per week pocket money, which earned him the newspaper title of

'Britain's richest schoolboy'. He was expelled from the school for posses-
sion of drugs and the same happened at his next school, Gordonstoun,
when a detective guarding fellow pupil Prince Andrew discovered drugs
in a hollow chair leg.

Through his twenties, Cos's drug abuse fuelled the newspaper gossip
columns. He even had a spell in the Betty Ford clinic. But it was not until
Cos discovered a passion for climbing that his drug problems appeared
to be behind him. He climbed Mont Blanc and then graduated to Cho
Oyu and on to Everest. I had the pleasure of knowing Cos the climber
during two expeditions. He was a very pleasant and likeable companion.
As a friend who also climbed with him said to me, 'what a daft way for
such a nice bloke to die.'

On the day after our reunion at Chris Brown's house, Mike Matthew's
parents met with Jon Tinker and other members of the OTT expedition
in Sheffield. It was always going to be a difficult meeting and it could well
have been the end of the issue, but no mention was made of the problems
with the oxygen. It still seemed that at this stage Mike's family, although
clearly grieving, seemed to accept that his was just another death on the
world's highest mountain.

It all changed some two months after the expedition ended, when the
Matthews family received a phone call from John Crellin, who had been a
member of the OTT expedition, saying that there had been a problem with
oxygen on the expedition. Subsequently, the Canadians, Denis Brown and
David Rodney, also contacted the Matthews family to make allegations
about the oxygen systems which Henry Todd had provided, confirming
that not all were the Poisk system which the OTT brochure promised
would be used on Everest.

The Matthews family started to ask questions and they were not happy
with the answers.

I was first contacted twenty months later in January 2001 by lawyers
representing the Matthews family, who asked if I would be willing to be

interviewed. I agreed, given that I felt that anything I said would absolve Jon Tinker and Mike Smith from any blame and also given that in my view the death had been a sad result of the dangers of climbing at over 8,000 metres. Whether or not the oxygen issue had in some way led to Mike's death was possible, but it was very unlikely that it could be proved.

At a second meeting with the lawyers, I mentioned that I would be willing to search for Mike's body while I was back on Everest in April of that year. I also pointed out that if the body hadn't been seen by expeditions on Everest before the pre-monsoon season in 2001, it would be very unlikely that we would find it and, most importantly, I wasn't prepared under any circumstances to risk lives to recover Mike's body.

I later met with the Matthews family at their home in London. It was a strange meeting because I sensed that the Matthews family saw me as potentially being a spy, given that some of the accused were close friends of mine. I simply saw myself as an honest broker who had had a very high opinion of their son and, as a father, I wanted to help them to achieve some closure.

Given the nature of the death, various people involved had clearly taken legal advice and lawyers had advised them not to say too much to the family. This had created an understandable impression that the mountaineers involved were working together to cover up issues. I am confident that this was not the case, but more openness and transparency, particularly during the meeting at the OTT office in June 1999, may well have brought the issues surrounding Mike's death to an earlier conclusion.

Because Martin Doyle and Nick Kekus were professional mountain guides, their professional governing body, the British Mountain Guides, carried out their own investigation and their professional standards committee concluded that there was no case to answer. This also didn't satisfy Mike's father who felt that this was simply a case of professionals protecting fellow professionals.

In effect, two camps were forming, on one side was the Matthews family, supported by disgruntled OTT clients, and on the other side the greater climbing community, who saw Mike's death simply as a consequence of the dangers of climbing at high altitude. The issue was not going to go away, as over a period of time the disgruntled clients of OTT, and others who had crossed paths with Henry Todd, used Mike's death as a way of getting back at a number of people for various issues which they had had in 1999 or before.

Eventually the Matthews family felt that they had no alternative but to turn to the law to get answers to the questions they felt were still unanswered, but it would take a number of years before the case reached court.

18

A SAD SEARCH

I had initially planned to be back in the Himalaya in 2000, and during a phone call one of my American clients said he was looking forward to climbing with me because he had heard that I liked to party. I acknowledge that I am not against the odd drink, but I have never been a party animal, and I asked how the client had heard about this. He said he had read it in a book written by the Swedish climber Göran Kropp. I asked him if he could fax me a copy of what Göran had written, which he duly did.

In the book Göran had written:

> I enjoyed life at Base Camp. I met old friends and made new ones, plus there were many funny characters. We lived between the Scotsman, Mike Trueman, who belonged to Mal Duff's expedition, and a group of soldiers from Serbia and Macedonia. Base Camp gossip said the soldiers were war criminals on the run who'd taken refuge here at the end of the world. Or, they'd been declared too crazy to fight – and had been exiled to Mount Everest. In any case, they certainly knew how to party, as did Mike.

He then went on to make bizarre claims that I was a 'wild, unkempt and slovenly drunkard'.

What Göran had done was mix up my name with another Mike who was our Base Camp manager, Mick Burns, and, to be fair, it was a fairly accurate description of Mick. I looked up 'libel lawyers' on the internet and contacted the first one I found. It was a very simple case and by the end of the week the publishers had admitted liability for the mistake and the book had been banned from being sold in the UK. I didn't even have to go to court – the libel lawyer did all the work and I was awarded £45,000 in damages.

By 2001, when I returned to Everest, I was living in Midhurst in West Sussex with my partner Jacqui, who would later become my wife. Only one year away from my fiftieth birthday, I was in the process of leaving full-time mountaineering and I saw this as a final trip to the Big Hill.

I had agreed in 2001 to work with Gary Guller, who was still attempting to be the first climber with only one arm to climb Everest – a feat he was to achieve two years later. On the way into Base Camp I was also going to be working with a UK TV crew who were making a documentary about events in 1999 – I just hoped it would be a fair and balanced programme without any credence being given to conspiracy theories.

On the route to the mountain we held a moving service at Mike Matthews' memorial chorten, which is on top of the Duglha Hill at the start of the valley leading up to Base Camp.

I won't go in to the day-to-day progress of that season, but there were some notable events. The first was the expedition leaders conference, which I attended on 13 April 2001. It should have lasted ten minutes and had it been filmed it would have made a good 'how not to run a meeting' video. I just sat there amused as larger and larger egos took the floor, while at the same time the rubbish being spoken was in direct proportion to the increasing noise made by each speaker making themselves heard. To me it very much looked like a new breed of Everest leaders were vying to make their mark, and I drew some comfort from my decision to change direction after this expedition.

There had been no sightings of Mike's body during the climbing seasons since 1999. As early as Saturday 14 April 2001 we had a very heavy snowfall at Base Camp and it already looked like the very slim chance we had of finding Mike's body had just got much slimmer. I also had an email that day from lawyers in the UK about the recovery of the body. My stance was simple, I was there as a mountaineer to find the body if I could, so that Mike's family could find peace. I certainly wasn't there to investigate a crime – that was a matter for the legal profession.

Although I was the technical leader, Gary had the contracts with the clients, one of whom had over-exaggerated his climbing CV and from day one at Base Camp was clearly out of his depth. The first time we went through the Icefall he arrived at Camp 1 some eight hours after me, which was far too long to be in the Icefall as after 9 a.m. the sun hits the ice and the Icefall becomes increasingly more dangerous. I sacked him on the spot, and even though he appealed to Gary, to whom he had paid his money, I refused to change my mind. He should not have been on the mountain and I only had his best interests at heart.

The weather continued to be strange, and although I managed over a week at Camp 2 acclimatising, we had regular reports during this time that below us Base Camp was being hit by snowstorms.

I had returned to Base Camp when, on 30 April, I heard the news that the legendary Babu Sherpa had been killed at Camp 2 the day before. At 4 p.m. he left his tent at Camp 2 on his own to do some filming and shortly afterwards he fell into a crevasse. His disappearance was discovered some time later, and after a long search his body was discovered just before midnight. His body was brought down later that day and I went over to the tent where he had been laid out to offer my respects by placing a Buddhist scarf on his body and by lighting a candle. He was a national hero and this was shown a week later when tens of thousands attended his funeral in Kathmandu. Babu's body was flown out of Base Camp on 1 May 2001, my forty-ninth birthday. As the helicopter lifted off I felt an amazing surge of sadness.

One climber who was sharing our permit, but who was not part of our team in 2001, had summited Everest in quick time the year before, but his Sherpa, who I knew well, told me the climber had used drugs to do this and his Sherpa was very worried that he was going to do the same again in 2001. Rumours that some climbers were using drugs had been circulating for some time. It probably should not have been surprising that drugs were being used, given that mountaineering is an endurance sport, but I was horrified. The climber had become particularly unwell when he had returned to the South Col the previous year after the effects of whatever he had used had worn off, and this was another concern for his Sherpa – that he may have to be rescued following further drug usage. Given the nature of the individual, who I had found to be a very unpleasant character to be around, I wasn't surprised to hear about the drugs, but I also felt very sad that a pastime which I loved had become so tainted.

I planned to go back up to Camp 2 on 9 May, but the weather quickly deteriorated first thing in the morning. We also heard later that there had been two collapses in the Icefall. From high on the mountain we also got reports of heavy snowfall and at last I came to the conclusion that while a summit attempt up the south-east ridge might become feasible, the conditions in the area where Mike's body was possibly located meant that any search would be far too dangerous – I called the search off. I went to Everest in the hope of finding Mike's body and to help a family find some peace, but sadly this was not now going to be achieved. I had found in the process that Everest was changing; new egos were emerging and the use of drugs had particularly saddened me – in terms of climbing it was time to bid Everest farewell.

19

GENOCIDE AND REGICIDE

From Everest, and my life as a mountaineer, I went almost immediately to work in Bosnia as director of an aid agency. Little had changed since I had worked in the war in the former Yugoslavia some eight years before. Hatred still existed between the ethnic groups, but my task was to rebuild homes that had been destroyed on both sides of the ethnic divide during the war, and to help displaced families to move back to their pre-war homes.

I headed up a multi-ethnic team who worked incredibly well together to rebuild their broken nation. There was little doubt that this would probably take decades to achieve, but a start had to be made.

In the middle of the area where I worked was Srebrenica, which had come to symbolise the horrors which had occurred in many places during the war. In 2001 it was still a battered village, but such things as the opening of a bakery, which my organisation had sponsored, were, bit by bit, helping the community to rebuild itself.

Again I went walking in the hills, which was now a bit safer than it had been when I was previously there as most of the minefields were now well marked.

Sarajevo remained a broken city. The old town was largely untouched, but towards the airport, and on the hills overlooking the city, there were constant reminders of the savagery of war. The most poignant lasting signs of what had taken place were the remains of the 1984 Winter Olympics. The large car park alongside the ice skating arena where Torvill and Dean won their figure skating gold medal had become an overused graveyard, while the banking of the bobsleigh track showed the marks of countless shell holes.

In many of the areas where we worked, mass graves were still being discovered and, where possible, every effort was being made to identify the dead. There was a strong rumour that overflights by aircraft using sophisticated equipment had identified all of the mass graves at the end of the war, but there would have been chaos if their locations had all been announced at the same time. The publication of their locations was, therefore, being drip fed year by year.

Despite all this, there was a determination that the country would not be allowed to slip backwards into a state of anarchy. One example was the return of skiers to the slopes above Sarajevo. It was not the finest skiing that I had ever experienced, and it was difficult to appreciate that, some nineteen years before, the greatest skiers in the world had hurtled down those slopes. The chairlifts were certainly the flimsiest I had ever used, but equipment can be easily changed – what was more important was the need to restore hope to the people of Bosnia, and the return of large numbers of skiers to the slopes was a symbol that some things were starting, albeit at a slow pace, to return to normal.

From Bosnia I moved back to the UK to become, at the age of fifty, director of operations for the largest school expedition company in the world – who were running over 400 expeditions each year to every corner of the globe.

The civil war in Bosnia officially ended in December 1995. It had gripped the interest of the world's media, largely because it was a European conflict. Only two months later, in February 1996, the civil war broke out in Nepal which was to last over ten years, but unlike the war in Bosnia, this conflict received only sketchy coverage from the world's media.

The war was launched in Nepal by Maoists in an attempt to establish a republic by overthrowing the Nepalese monarchy. During the ten years of the conflict it is estimated that over 15,000 Nepalese were killed and, to put this into some context, during the forty years of the Troubles in Northern Ireland, just under 3,600 were killed.

What now seems bizarre in retrospect is that while the war was being fought expeditions to the high mountains remained largely unaffected. There was the very odd incident, but the impact on trekkers was far more noticeable, because the Maoists often stopped trekking groups to demand that they contributed towards the Maoist cause.

The biggest contributor to the Maoist cause, although he wasn't aware that he would be at the time, was Crown Prince Dipendra who, on 1 June 2001, shot dead nine members of the royal family including his mother and father, the king and queen, before shooting himself. For a nation that literally worshipped their king, this was an enormous tragedy.

It took Dipendra four days to die, during which time he was technically the king following the death of his father. Had he survived, having committed regicide, infanticide, fratricide and patricide, there is no doubt that the country would have been plunged into a constitutional crisis, but his suicide had prevented this. Gyanendra, Dipendra's uncle, succeeded him as the king.

Gyanendra was a particularly unpopular monarch, and his son Prince Paras, by now the crown prince, was even more unpopular than his father, having previously been accused of murdering a popular Nepalese singer. He was despised by the Nepalese for his playboy lifestyle, which I witnessed in 2007 when I was heading up a UN team to verify the status of Maoist combatants. I was at a meeting at a hotel in Kathmandu when a clearly drunken Prince Paras strolled over to introduce himself with two Western girls hanging on to his arms, with his wife following on sedately behind.

In 2005, the king suspended the constitution and assumed direct authority for governing the country. This was another home goal by the royal family, which made the monarchy even less popular, while at the same time increasing support for the Maoist cause. In the face of broad opposition he restored the previous government, and his reign officially ended two years later when the government declared Nepal to be a republic and abolished the monarchy.

20

EVEREST IN THE DOCK

The Matthews' legal case had slowly progressed since 1999, and in 2006 a private prosecution reached court, seven years after Mike's death.

I had not been involved directly in the case or its issues since I returned from Everest in 2001. I had been asked to be a witness, but although there was some circumstantial evidence, I didn't believe that it was compelling enough to bring a guilty verdict against any of the defendants. Climbing Everest was, is, and will always be, inherently dangerous, and irrespective of how much client climbers are willing to pay there can never be any guarantee that others will be responsible for their safety. Ultimately, every climber on Everest needs to be experienced enough to be responsible for their own safety.

The four defendants in the case were Jon Tinker, Henry Todd, Mike Smith and Alpine Mountaineering Limited, which was the new name of OTT, which was already in liquidation, having previously reached an out of court settlement with the Matthews family. A number of OTT's clients were due to be called as witnesses, including Dave Rodney, John Crellin and Katja Staartjes. That Dave and John were involved didn't overly surprise me. John appeared to be the weakest member of the OTT team in 1999 and it was always unlikely that he was going to reach the summit. He also simply didn't seem to fit in with the rest of the team and he never seemed to have formed a close relationship with the team leaders. I met him on the walk-out after the expedition and I very much got the impression that he felt he had wasted the money he had paid to attempt to climb Everest.

Dave also didn't get on with Jon Tinker or Nick, and whenever I saw him on the mountain I always got the impression that he felt that he was an individual who thought he was a bit special, rather than a member of a team. This was reflected at the South Col where Dave was insistent that he only got Poisk oxygen, rather than take whatever he was given (which other team members accepted), which resulted in an argument between him and Nick.

The allegations against the accused were:

- There was a lack of safety briefings, Sherpa support for Mike, and a lack of radios.
- The oxygen cylinders were faulty.
- Mike Smith failed to stay in contact with Mike, didn't short-rope him, and failed to ensure that Mike didn't become lost between the end of the fixed ropes and the Balcony.

The allegations also stated that 'Todd is perhaps the most criminally negligent of all.'

To be fair, Henry Todd had not intentionally supplied oxygen bottles in 1999 which were not fit for purpose. He made his money from supplying useable oxygen and it was in his interests for the systems to work. That said, not having a Plan B was in my view questionable, and the decision to distribute the oxygen over the mountain before telling teams that there was a major issue was reprehensible.

There was no doubt that Henry's colourful and indeed criminal past was not going to do him any favours. He had been jailed for two years for theft and fraud, followed by thirteen years for being one of the two big players in, at the time, Britain's biggest ever drugs bust. He had been banned from entering Nepal by the Nepalese Ministry of Tourism for two years when in 2000 he had a fight with an American reporter at Base Camp, and a magazine article calling him the 'Toddfather' did nothing to enhance his reputation.

There was also a strange allegation being made by Thomas Sjögren, who with his wife Tina had formed their own expedition in 1999. In their evidence they said that as soon as the storm cleared after we had reached the summit on 13 May, Henry had climbed up the mountain as far as the South Col, which was unusual as Henry rarely went above Camp 2. Reports from Base Camp suggested that Henry had gone as high as 8,200 metres and when he returned down the mountain he told Thomas Sjögren that there was no point in his expedition attempting to reach the summit, because there was waist-deep snow above the South Col. Henry also threatened to close the Icefall (remove the ladders which formed the bridges across the crevasses). Thomas and Tina ignored Henry's advice and found no evidence of the snow being too deep as they made a successful climb to the summit.

I left Henry at Camp 2 on 15 May 1999 and I had departed from Base Camp by the time he descended and had his conversation with Thomas. In my diary at the time I expressed sympathy for the climbers on Henry's Lhotse permit because I had heard that prior to my departure from Base Camp on 17 May Henry had called off their expedition, which seemed very bizarre. They were not paying as much as the clients on Everest, but climbing Lhotse was still relatively expensive and given that there were almost two weeks left before their permit ran out, I couldn't understand at all why Henry had 'pulled the plug' on his clients.

It is not overly surprising that all the witnesses for the prosecution had previously had their own issues with OTT or Henry Todd.

Climbing on Everest by its very nature is dangerous. In my view every climber who attempts the mountain must have enough experience to look after themselves in bad weather. Whilst it might be possible to guide climbers with less experience at lower levels on the mountain in most weather conditions, it is simply not possible to guide in bad weather high on the mountain. Guides are human and vulnerable, as we found in 1996 when three of the five climbers who died on the Nepalese side of the mountain were qualified mountain guides.

Climbers who want to reach the summit of Everest must accept responsibility for their actions. That there were no Sherpas with Mike Matthews is somewhat questionable given that seven Sherpas from OTT summited that day, together with six OTT clients and guides, but this was not necessarily a sign of negligence, given that Sherpas are assigned to a number of tasks besides looking after other climbers, including fixing and clearing ropes.

Mike Matthews and Mike Smith summited at a time which should have given them plenty of time during daylight to make it safely down to the South Col.

Mike Smith was an experienced climber but he was also human. The weather had already started to deteriorate while he and Mike Matthews were still high on the mountain. Suggesting that Mike Smith should have short-roped Mike Matthews assumes that Mike Smith was in a far better physical state. I certainly would not have been able to short-rope anyone else when I was at the same point some three hours before the two Mikes – I felt shattered.

In my view, taking account of the available evidence, Mike Smith did all he could have done to look after Mike Matthews and given the deteriorating weather conditions, Mike Smith was very lucky to have survived.

In terms of the briefings – this is Everest. It is not a place for lessons in mountaineering. It doesn't mean that climbers can't be coached during the early phases of an expedition, but given that the OTT climbers had already been to the South Col before they returned there on 12 May, it is reasonable to assume that they knew what to expect and I certainly didn't hear any complaints about there not having been any briefings. I had visited OTT many times during the expedition and been with them on the mountain and I never got the impression that the team members were anything other than well-informed. I had also been on the same mountain on at least two previous occasions with Jon Tinker and Nick Kekus and I had great professional respect for both of them.

The problems with oxygen in the end could not be hidden, although it would have been useful to be made aware of them as soon as Henry knew there was an issue. It was certainly a very questionable decision to distribute the oxygen cylinders all over the mountain before informing all of the teams that there was a problem. There did seem to be a high incidence of oxygen equipment failure – I had two cylinders which didn't work during my summit climb, but there is no statistical evidence to show that the oxygen problems in the end were greater than normal – it wasn't until changes were made to the breathing systems in the early 2000s that reliability significantly increased.

The most significant implication was that Mike Matthews' death was in some way a result of him using a faulty oxygen system, but this was always going to be extremely difficult, if not impossible, to prove.

The climbing world eagerly awaited the verdict. The judge described Mike Matthews as, 'an exceptional young man, a man of courage and determination', a statement that those who had the privilege of knowing Mike would wholeheartedly agree with. The judge went on to say that he felt it was 'hardly tolerable' that a criminal charge had been brought against Michael Smith, who in attempting to stay with Mike Matthews had risked his own life.

Perhaps in view of the obvious issues with oxygen, the Matthews family might have felt that this was an area where their lawyers would make inroads against the defendants, but the judge said that the prosecution case depended on pure and wholly impermissible speculation.

The judge concluded by saying, 'It is not the purpose of the criminal law to stifle the spirit of adventure, or inhibit personal ambition and endeavour; it would be most regrettable if the serious crime of manslaughter might be seen as a cloud, constantly hanging over those old enough to decide how they wish to live their lives.'

The judge then dismissed all charges against the defendants.

Perversely two books then appeared about 'Operation Julie', which was at the time still the UK's biggest drugs bust, and resulted in Henry Todd, as one of the two big players in the drugs ring, receiving a thirteen-year prison sentence. It is not clear if the publishing of the books was a coincidence given that Operation Julie dated from the 1970s, or whether it was a result of the publicity surrounding the Matthews court case. It made little impact, however, on Henry Todd, who went back to supplying oxygen to Everest expeditions.

Of those who were there in 1999, the New Zealand summiteer Ray Brown died three years later at the age of fifty-one after a training run. That same year, two more climbers who were on Everest in 1996 also died. Euan Duncan died in a flying accident at the age of thirty-nine, after transferring to the Australian Air Force, and Göran Kropp was killed at the age of thirty-six while climbing in the US. In 2009 John Crellin, who had been a witness in the Mike Matthews case, died in a motorcycle accident while racing on the Isle of Man at the age of fifty-five.

Everest is dangerous, it requires commitment and men and women will always want to challenge themselves by climbing it. It should not be surprising that so many of those who climb on its slopes subsequently die at relatively young ages while challenging themselves in other ways.

Everest is not technically difficult, but its enormous size will always mean that climbing the mountain is a challenge that has significant risks. Even the most experienced high altitude guides have died on the mountain, which demonstrates that skill alone cannot eliminate the risks. But, as the world's highest mountain, it will always be a summit which climbers will want to reach. It is an individual's responsibility to gain the necessary experience before attempting the mountain, and if things do go wrong it is wrong to expect others to get a climber out of a bad situation – particularly when they are also fighting for their own lives.

Everest will always be a challenge – because it is there.

POSTSCRIPT

THE NEW EVEREST

At 6.45 a.m. on 18 April 2014 an enormous chunk of ice broke free from the glacier on the western shoulder of Everest.

Some three hours earlier at Base Camp, Sherpas from a number of expeditions had crawled out of their cosy sleeping bags into the inhospitably cold atmosphere that pervades Everest Base Camp before dawn. After a warming hot drink and some snatched nourishment they then helped each other to lift enormous loads on to their backs, loads which had been packed the evening before. They then adjusted the straps around their foreheads which were tied to their packs, which historically is the way Sherpas have carried loads for centuries, before moving off into the cold pre-dawn light. The Sherpas didn't say much, as dozens of them started to grind their way up through the Icefall. This was just another work day on Everest and the Sherpas needed to establish and supply the higher camps so that the hundreds of clients, amongst a growing number of commercial climbing companies, could then move up and sleep and eat at camps 1 and 2 and so start their acclimatisation process.

The huge loads the Sherpas were carrying made them move very slowly and they had to stop at intervals to pace their efforts and to gain some respite. By the time they reached an area in the Icefall known as the 'Popcorn Field' they were moving in a long line, aching from the exertion, with heads bowed, looking down at the back of the legs of the Sherpa in front of them.

The large block of ice which had broken off the western shoulder hurtled across the upper reaches of the Icefall and smashed into the long line of Sherpas. Several must have died instantly, while others were buried under snow and ice. Within a very short space of time, sixteen Sherpas had perished and many others were injured, doing what they did to make a living to support themselves and their families. In a fleeting moment many lives were extinguished and the avalanche resulted in the largest single death toll from any accident on Everest.

Climbing has always been commercial given that it has always been expensive to mount expeditions to the Himalayan peaks. Organisations such as the Royal Geographical Society supported the early expeditions to Everest, but it then became the norm to seek companies to provide the funds to pay for expeditions, such as the 1975 British South-West Face Expedition which was sponsored by Barclays Bank. The funding was provided to achieve success and, therefore, only the climbing elite had the opportunity to climb the Himalayan giants. In the 1980s this changed somewhat with an increase in the number of small expeditions seeking to climb hard routes on mountains that few outside the mountaineering fraternity had heard of.

The commercial climbing period as we know it started to come into being from 1990 and its evolution since then has depended on four groups: the Nepalese government, who want to make money by creating a permit system; the commercial companies who run the expeditions, who need a certain number of clients to make their operation commercially viable; the Sherpas who do the vast majority of work on the mountains; and the client climbers who fund the system.

Historically, it is the government of Nepal who has been the most dominant of the four groups, but they have to maintain a system which allows commercial companies to operate and make a profit and, to some extent, companies have a certain amount of influence – some cynics might suggest that in part this influence has had to be paid for. In addition, the commercial companies have to be able to keep prices at a level to attract the necessary number of climbers each year and statistics indicate that they have been successful in doing this.

The last group, the Sherpas, have the least amount of power within the four interested parties. Nepal is a very poor nation and although Sherpas are relatively well paid compared with the average national income, they are not well paid when the profits of the climbing companies for whom they work are taken into account.

There had been an argument, some would describe it as a brawl, at Camp 2 in 2013 involving Sherpas and some Western climbers and in 2014 the Nepal Ministry of Tourism, as the government body responsible for mountaineering in the country, decided to base officials at Everest Base Camp. Following the avalanche on 18 April, a meeting was held at Base Camp attended by expedition and Sherpa leaders, but the ministry officials were nowhere to be seen.

In the early years of commercial climbing, companies were generally Western-owned and run, but over the years the number of Nepalese-owned commercial ventures has grown. This has been good for Nepal, but it has also made the Sherpas more aware of the relatively large amounts of money which were being made by both the government and the expedition organisers when all of the hard work on the mountains – much of it in very dangerous conditions – was being done by the Sherpas for a comparative pittance.

This avalanche was an awful tragedy which was going to become a significant crossroads in the development of climbing on the mountain.

If Everest could be climbed without a permit or the use of a commercial company it would cost roughly US$4,000 for clothing and personal climbing equipment, $1,000 for food, $1,000 for oxygen and another $1,000 to get the climber and kit to Base Camp – a total of $7,000. The commercial climbing companies in 2014 tended to charge on average some $60,000. Clothing and personal climbing equipment was not included, but food, oxygen and the journey to Base Camp was covered which amounts to, say, $3,000. The question is, where did the additional $57,000 go?

$10,000 was paid per person to the Nepal Government for the Everest permit and, being generous, another $2,000 per client went towards other government fees, such as the cost of clothing and paying for the liaison officer, which each expedition had to have – leaving a remainder of $45,000 left to be accounted for. Some $1,000 per person went towards paying for mountain guides, while another $1,000 went towards the cost of fixing the Icefall with ladders and ropes and another $1,000 paid for the fixed ropes between camps on the mountain. The ropes along the route and the cost of maintaining the route through the Icefall are generally shared between expeditions.

Of the remaining $42,000 it would be over-generous to say that $10,000 per person would go towards the costs of Sherpas and camp staff, but even erring on the side of caution, expeditions who charged $60,000 to climb Everest were making a gross profit based on ten clients of around $320,000.

At the same time, the Nepalese government was making huge sums from simply issuing permits, whereas the Sherpas who do all of the hard work and take the risks were likely to receive about $3,000–$6,000 per expedition, and for those killed in the avalanche their families would get a reported $10,000 each.

Part of the fees which commercial climbing expeditions pay to the government of Nepal goes towards insuring the Sherpas against injury or death. The amount payable in 2014 in the event of death had been more than doubled, but at $10,000 per Sherpa it was only the equivalent of about two years of work and many who died were young, with decades of earning potential ahead of them.

Furthermore, it was said that there were 330 climbers on Everest in the spring of 2014, which would have earned the Nepalese government some $3,000,000 in revenue just for the issuing of the climbing permits.

It can be argued that commercial companies are charging too much, but to be fair to them the prices haven't changed much since 1996. What has changed is the huge growth in climbers who want to reach the summit of Everest – something commercial companies can exploit, and this can be shown using the British as an example.

British climbers first reached the summit of Everest in 1975 and, with only one more successful expedition taking place during that decade, by the end of the 1970s the total number of British ascents stood at six (Mick Burke who died in 1975 is not listed as an official summiteer but I have added him to the total). During the 1980s a further three British climbers summited and this was added to in the 1990s by an additional thirty-four, bringing the total of British climbers who had summited Everest before 2000 to forty-three (of these, three climbers had reached the summit for a second time).

During the next ten years, a further 168 British climbers reached the summit (with some making more than one ascent, bringing the number of British ascents during the period to 194), almost four times the number of climbers who got to the top in the first twenty-four years. It is also worthy of note that between 2000 and 2004, only thirty-seven British climbers were successful, but in the same five-year period from 2005 to 2009 a further 131 Britons reached the summit. Commercial climbing on Everest had become established and there were clearly lots of clients seeking to reach the top of the world.

Another question which needs to be addressed is: has the mountain become more dangerous in line with the increase in successful summits? Again, using the British as an example and looking at the period between 1975 and 2009, a total of twelve British climbers had died on Everest. During the period 1975 to 1999, there were nine deaths with forty-three individuals reaching the summit. Or, looking at it in another way, a death to summit ratio of 1:4.7. But in the next decade when there were 168 British climbers reaching the summit there were only three deaths, or a ratio of 1:56.

Although the number of expeditions also increased significantly from 2000 to 2009, the number of Sherpas who died in that decade was eight, less than half of the number killed between 1990 and 1999, when there were far fewer expeditions attempting to climb Everest.

I would be the first to look beyond statistics for answers, but in simple terms the risks of climbing Everest appear to have been significantly reduced.

This is hardly surprising given that commercial expeditions have been focusing on one route each on the north and south sides of the mountain. The nuances of the routes and the weather patterns which indicate when it is the best time to go for the summit have become well known – but what will never be mastered is the ice, rock and snow which make up the giant that is Everest. The risk that climbers could be in the wrong place at the wrong time has always and will always be a gamble that no amount of experience can influence, and the avalanche that cost the huge loss of life on 18 April 2014 was a costly reminder that nothing is guaranteed for those who climb Everest.